Tune thy Musicke to thy Hart
The Art of Eloquent Singing in England, 1597–1622

Many singers today perform Elizabethan and Jacobean lute-songs, but until now no book has addressed the concerns of these performers. In this practical, illustrated guide Robert Toft outlines the principles which governed song performance and composition in the early seventeenth century, and shows how these historical principles may be used to move and delight modern audiences.

The main purpose of early seventeenth-century singing was to persuade listeners by using a style of utterance that had two principal parts – to sing eloquently and to act aptly. Toft discusses these two facets of singing within a broad cultural context, drawing upon music's sister arts, poetry and oratory, to establish the nature of eloquence and action in relation to singing. He concentrates on those techniques which can be transferred easily from one medium to the other. Specifically, he draws on the two aspects of oratory which directly bear on singing: elocution – the methods of amplifying and decorating poetry and music with figures – and pronunciatio – techniques of making figurative language inflame the passions of the listeners.

The arrangement of the material has been inspired by the method of schooling William Kempe prescribed in 1588. The first part of the book examines *elocutio*, for singers need to understand the structure of the songs before they can sing them well. The second part considers *pronunciatio* and focuses on the techniques used to capture and inflame the minds of the listeners, that is, the role of punctuation in utterance, the methods for making figures and other passionate ornaments manifest, the application of divisions and graces to melodies, and the art of gesture. In the final section, Toft applies the techniques of early seventeenth-century eloquent delivery to two songs – 'Sorrow sorrow stay' and 'In darknesse let mee dwell' – by the great English songwriter John Dowland.

Robert Toft teaches at the Sydney Conservatorium of Music. He is author of *Aural Images of Lost Traditions: Sharps and Flats in the Sixteenth Century*.

T0317046

TUNE THY
‹ MUSICKE ›
TO THY HART

The Art of Eloquent Singing in England
1597–1622

ROBERT TOFT

UNIVERSITY OF TORONTO PRESS
TORONTO BUFFALO LONDON

© University of Toronto Press Incorporated 1993

Reprinted in 2018

Toronto Buffalo London
Printed in Canada
ISBN 0-8020-2848-9
ISBN 978-1-4875-7354-6 (paper)

Printed on acid-free paper

Canadian Cataloguing in Publication Data

Toft, Robert
  Tune thy musicke to thy hart

  Includes bibliographical references and index.
  ISBN 0-8020-2848-9

  1. Performance practice (Music) – 17th century
  2. Singing – Interpretation (Phrasing, dynamics, etc.)
  I. Title

ML 457.t75 1993   783'.046'0942   092-095508 1-7

Book design by Counterpunch/Linda Gustafson

This book has been published with the help of a grant from the
Canadian Federation for the Humanities, using funds provided
by the Social Sciences and Humanities Research Council of Canada.

✣ CONTENTS

✤ ACKNOWLEDGMENTS

I wish to thank all those people who made it possible for me to write this book. The need for a book such as this one became apparent to me more than a decade ago when, as an accompanist, I began coaching singers who, like me, were searching for ways of approaching English lute-songs of the late sixteenth and early seventeenth centuries from within the culture of the period. In this endeavour, a number of singers, colleagues, and friends have been a great help to me. To all those students over the years who persevered and mastered, to a greater or lesser degree, the art of eloquent singing as I believe it was practised in the early seventeenth century, I owe a great debt of gratitude, for they provided me with the kind of workshop a researcher in this area needs. At the end of a lengthy process of putting principles derived from treatises of the period into practice, this book emerged. Robert Spencer, working separately along similar lines, most generously supplied me not only with information he had gleaned from the plays of Shakespeare but also with the engraving which graces the cover of this book. Richard Rastall read the manuscript carefully and made a number of useful suggestions for its improvement. Any errors, omissions, or misinterpretations of the material used in this study remain, of course, my own responsibility. To the Faculty of Graduate

Studies at the University of Western Ontario, I extend my gratitude for various grants which facilitated the production of this book. And finally, I thank Margaret, Korin, Kira, and Aidan, as well as my parents, for their constant support and encouragement.

Portions of this study originally appeared in 'Musicke a sister to Poetrie: Rhetorical Artifice in the Passionate Airs of John Dowland,' *Early Music* 12 (1984) 190–9 © Oxford University Press, and the passages concerned are used by permission.

Tune thy Musicke to thy Hart

The Art of Eloquent Singing in England

1597–1622

 INTRODUCTION

Although attitudes toward the performance of music from earlier cultures have changed greatly in the past twenty or thirty years, the performer's task, or at least the task of those performers who are interested in performance from an historical perspective, remains the same. If we wish to re-create performing practices of these cultures, we must extrapolate from historical documents to bridge the gap that exists between those documents and actual performance. The further the culture is from our time, the more difficult the problem, especially when, to take the historical period of this book as an example, it might seem at first glance that English society at the beginning of the seventeenth century is simply an earlier form of our own culture. On closer examination, however, we realize that it is, in fact, quite a different culture. Obviously, musical style and the aesthetic underlying that style have changed markedly in the past four hundred years, and this makes us foreigners in late Elizabethan and Jacobean society. It is probably safe to assume that we do not have an intuitive understanding of the music from this period or of approaches to its performance, and in order to recover the performing practices of the early seventeenth century, we must reconstruct those practices from the artefacts which survive, that is, from the music itself and from both musical and non-musical treatises. Above all, we must take care to thicken the context of our discussion and place musical activity in its broader cultural perspective. By doing this, we can at least make an attempt to avoid, to use the words of the historian Robin Collingwood, the 'mistake of arranging in the past what is actually all present experience.'[1]

In late sixteenth- and early seventeenth-century England, music was closely related to its sister arts poetry and oratory, all three of these arts being pervasively influenced by rhetoric. Statements connecting the arts of rhetoric and music occur with increasing frequency between the sixteenth and the eighteenth centuries. In fact, by the early seventeenth century, the connection had become so well established that Henry Peacham the Younger, in *The Compleat Gentleman* (London 1622), was able to begin the section devoted to the place of music in a gentleman's life with the words 'Musicke a sister to Poetrie.' The prominent position afforded these words reaffirms the link between rhetoric and music which was in Europe by this time at least two centuries old.[2] Peacham was not content merely to mention superficial similarities, however, and in the course of his discussion of music, he stated precisely what some of the links between poetry and music were: 'Yea, in my opinion, no Rhetoricke more perswadeth, or hath greater power over the mind; nay, hath not Musicke her figures, the same which Rhetorique? What is a *Revert* but her *Antistrophe?* her reports, but sweete *Anaphora's?* her counterchange of points, *Antimetabole's?* her passionate Aires but *Prosopopoea's?* with infinite other of the same nature' (p 103). Other writers commented upon the close connections between poetry and music as well. Francis Bacon contended that 'there be in *Musick* certaine *Figures*, or *Tropes*; almost agreeing with the *Figures* of *Rhetoricke*; And with the *Affections* of the *Minde*, and other *Senses*' (1627 p 38), and Thomas Campion asserted that in songs music enhances the persuasive qualities of the text:

> Happy is hee whose words can move,
> Yet sweet Notes help perswasion.
> Mixe your words with Musicke then,
> That they the more may enter.
> (1614, no 5)

As Peacham, Bacon, and Campion clearly demonstrate, in early seventeenth-century England the main goal of music, along with its sister arts oratory and poetry, was to persuade or move the mind, that is, the affections or passions, of the listener. Passions, to quote Thomas Wilson, 'are none other thyng, but a stirryng, or forcyng of the mynde, either to desier, or elles to detest, and lothe any thyng, more vehemently then by nature we are commonly wonte to doe' (1553 p 266). This increased vehemence, notes Thomas Wright, is caused by certain internal acts or operations of the soul which stir in the mind and alter the humours of the body. Affections, Wright observes, are things such as love, pain, ire, joy, fear, hope, flight, hatred, etc (1604 pp 8, 33–4).

The concept of the affections or passions and the discipline of rhetoric were inseparable in the late sixteenth and early seventeenth centuries.[3] Thomas Elyot defined rhetoric as 'the science, wherby is taughte an artificiall fourme of spekyng, wherin is the power to perswade, move, and delyte' (1546 f 41v), and textbooks on the subject were numerous. Writers dealt fully with the construction of impassioned discourse and the various devices one could use to capture the minds of listeners. Traditionally, the art of rhetoric was divided into five areas: *inventio, dispositio, elocutio* or *decoratio, memoria,* and *pronunciatio. Inventio* entailed finding the subject matter, and in *dispositio,* the material was ordered or arranged to serve the writer's purposes. Once the material was arranged, *elocutio* involved amplifying and decorating the poetry with fine words and sentences. The discourse then was memorized *(memoria)* and delivered, *pronunciatio* being concerned with the techniques of delivery orators employed to move the passions of listeners.

Within these five areas, some sixteenth-century English rhetoricians considered *pronunciatio* to be pre-eminent. Thomas Wilson's remarks are typical: 'Demosthenes therfore, that famouse Oratour beyng asked what was the chiefest point in al Oratorie, gave the chiefe and onely praise to Pronunciation, being demaunded, what was the seconde, and the thirde, he still made answere, Pronunciation, and would make none other aunswere ... For though a manne can finde out good matter, and good woordes, though he canne handsomely set them together, and cary them very well awaie in his mynde, yet it is to no purpose, if he have no utter-

aunce [delivery] ... Arte without utteraunce can dooe nothyng, utteraunce without Arte can dooe right muche' (1553 pp 33, 432). But, of
course, by Thomas Wilson's day the attributes of persuasive delivery had
been known for centuries. Quintilian (first century AD), for example, not
only mentioned the characteristics of good reading but also indicated
how important a knowledge of *elocutio* was to the orator in preparing his
delivery:[4] '[In reading aloud,] there is much that can only be taught in
actual practice, as for instance when the boy should take breath, at what
point he should introduce a pause into a line, where the sense ends or
begins, when the voice should be raised or lowered, what modulation
should be given to each phrase, and when he should increase or slacken
speed, or speak with greater or less energy. In this portion of my work I
will give but one golden rule: to do all these things, he must understand
what he reads' (I pp 146–7). In other words, in order to speak eloquently
one must understand the structure of the text and use the techniques of
pronunciatio (some of which Quintilian lists) to impress the figurative
language of the text *(elocutio)* upon listeners. In fact, *pronunciatio* and *elocutio* had become so closely related by the early seventeenth century that
Thomas Heywood (1612 f c4r) was able to declare that one of the reasons rhetoric was so important to actors was because it taught them how
to fit their pronunciation to the phrase (and by 'phrase' Heywood presumably meant *elocutio)*. The function of *pronunciatio* and *elocutio*, and
hence the goal of persuasive discourse, then, was to imprint the affections of the text in the souls of the listeners (Wright 1604 p 124).

   The art of eloquent speaking[5] in England during the sixteenth and
early seventeenth centuries presupposed a knowledge of *elocutio* and *pronunciatio*, and in some quarters, speaking and singing were viewed as arts
which were closely related. Roger Ascham (1545), for example, maintained that preachers and lawyers should receive instruction in singing so
that they would learn how to adapt their voices to the affections present
in their texts:

> Preachers and lawiers, bycause they shalnot without this
> [singinge], be able to rule their brestes, for every purpose.
> For where is no distinction in telling glad thinges and fear-

full thinges, gentilnes & cruelnes, softenes and vehe-
mentnes, and suche lyke matters, there can be no great perswasion. For the hearers, as Tullie sayeth, be muche affec-
tioned, as he is that speaketh. At his wordes be they
drawen, yf he stande still in one facion, their mindes stande
still with hym: If he thundre, they quake: If he chyde, they
feare: If he complayne, they sory with hym: and finally,
where a matter is spoken, with an apte voyce, for everye affection, the hearers for the moste parte, are moved as the
speaker woulde. But when a man is alwaye in one tune, lyke
an Humble bee, or els nowe up in the top of the churche,
nowe downe that no manne knoweth where to have hym:
or piping lyke a reede, or roring lyke a bull, as some
lawyers do, whiche thinke they do best, when they crye
lowdest, these shall never greatly moove, as I have knowen
many wel learned, have done, bicause theyr voyce was not
stayed afore, with learnyng to synge. (1 f 11v)

Somewhat later, William Byrd, in listing the reasons why everyone
should learn to sing, proclaimed that singing 'is the best meanes to pro-
cure a perfect pronunciation [delivery], and to make a good Orator' (1588
preface).

And in other countries, the arts of speaking and singing were inter-
twined as well. Both Italian and German writers advise singers to use the
orator as a model. Nicola Vicentino (1555) expresses the relationship
between the two arts explicitly:

La esperienza, dell'Oratore l'insegna, che si vede il modo
che tiene nell'Oratione, che hora dice forte, & hora piano,
& più tardo, & più presto, e con questo muove assai gl'oditori, & questo modo di muovere la misura, fa effetto assai
nell'animo, & per tal ragione si canterà la Musica alla
mente per imitar gli accenti, & effetti delle parti dell'oratione, & che effetto faria l'Oratore che recitasse una bella
oratione senza l'ordine di i suoi accenti, & pronuntie, &

moti veloci, & tardi, & con il dir piano & forte quello non muoveria gl'oditori. Il simile dè essere nella Musica. perche se l'Oratore muove gli oditori con gl'ordini sopradetti, quanto maggiormente la Musica recitata con i medesimi ordini accompagnati dall'Armonia, ben unita, farà molto più effetto / The experience of the orator teaches this [the value of changing tempo within a song (mutare misura)], for one sees how he proceeds in an oration – now he speaks loudly and now softly, and slower and faster, and with this greatly moves his auditors. This way of changing the tempo [muovere la misura] has a great effect on the soul, and for this reason, one shall sing the music in mind so as to imitate the accents and effects of the parts of an oration. What effect would an orator make by reciting a beautiful oration without arranging his accents and pronunciation, quicker and slower movements, and softer and louder speech? That would not move his auditors. The same should occur in music, for if the orator moves his auditors with the methods mentioned above, how much more would music, recited with the same methods, accompanied by harmony well united, make a greater effect. (1555 IV 42, f 94v)

In 1619, Michael Praetorius reaffirms the close connections between speaking and singing:

Gleich wie eines Oratoris Ampt ist / nicht allein eine Oration mit schönen anmutigen lebhafftigen Worten / unnd herrlichen Figuris zu zieren / sondern auch recht zu pronunciiren, und die affectus zu moviren: In dem er bald die Stimmen erhebet / bald sinken lesset / bald mit mächtiger und sanffter / bald mit ganzer und voller Stimme redet: Also ist eines Musicanten nicht allein singen / besondern künstlich und anmütig singen: Damit das herz der Zuhörer gerühret / und die affectus beweget werden / und also der Gesang seine Endschafft / dazu er gemacht / und

dahin er gerichtet / erreichen möge / Just as the concern of
an orator is not only to adorn an oration with beautiful,
pleasant, and vivid words and magnificent figures but also
to pronounce correctly [that is, to use good delivery] and to
move the affections: now he raises his voice, now he lets it
fall, now he speaks with a voice sometimes intense and soft,
sometimes whole and full: so must a musician not only sing
but sing with art and grace so that the heart of the listener
is stirred and the affections are moved, and thus the song
may achieve the purpose for which it was made and toward
which it is directed. (1619 p 229)

Ascham, Vicentino, and Praetorius make it clear that the main purpose of both singing and speaking was to move the affections of listeners. Singers, we learn, made the passions of the poem manifest through
their persuasive delivery and used many of the same techniques as orators to inflame and capture the minds of their listeners. But in order to
move the passions of others, a singer literally had to tune his music to
his heart, for the heart was 'the very seate of all Passions.' And if one
intended to 'imprint a passion in another, it is requisit first it be stamped
in our hearts: for thorow our voices, eies; and gestures, the world will
pierce and thorowly perceive how we are affected.' In other words, these
external actions of voice and gesture were regarded as the windows
through which listeners passed to 'discover the secret affections of
anothers heart' (Wright 1604 pp 33, 172, 174).

My purpose in this book is to extrapolate from historical documents,
both musical and non-musical, in order to re-create the style of song
delivery known in England between 1597 and 1622, the years which
mark the publication of the first and last books of lute-songs. My
approach to re-creating the environment in which the performers of
lute-songs operated stems from two questions I asked myself: 'What
would a listener in England have expected from a singer?' and 'Is it possible at this great distance to determine with some degree of accuracy
what those expectations would have been?' The answer to the latter
question is yes, but only if we look broadly in the culture for informa-

tion. In reconstructing performing practices, I like to use the analogy of concentric circles. The innermost circle contains the song one intends to perform, but since the sources of lute-songs offer no commentary on questions of phrasing, articulation, tempo, dynamics, tonal quality of the voice, etc, we must look to the next circle (writings about music) for information. Unfortunately, music treatises are almost as frustrating for us in this regard as are the sources of the music themselves, and we must proceed to the next circle. In this circle, I place those documents which deal with spoken discourse, the performing art that is the most closely related to singing. And it is here that we find the information which allows us to reconstruct early seventeenth-century principles of eloquent singing. The question we need ask at this point is 'Should information from an outer circle be applied to the centre?' I would answer this question affirmatively, because the observations of Ascham, Byrd, Vicentino, and Praetorius quoted above suggest that speaking and singing were arts which shared many of the same characteristics. Moreover, the teaching of rhetoric and oration was at the heart of grammar-school education, and from the time they were quite young, educated people in early seventeenth-century England, including singers, would have studied the principles of eloquent delivery from books on rhetoric and oration.[6]

Initially, we must learn to understand poems and their musical settings in the same way that English schoolchildren were taught to understand poetry, orations, etc; that is, we must learn to recognize 'every trope, every figure, aswell of words as of sentences' (Kempe 1588 p 233), taking note of the 'Rhetoricall placing of the words' (Brinsley 1612 p 104). Having achieved this, we will then be in a position to discover 'the Rhetoricall pronounciation and gesture fit for every word, sentence, and affection' (Kempe 1588 p 233). By subdividing the topic into these two categories, *elocutio* and *pronunciatio*, I am following traditional rhetorical teaching, a method I have found to be most useful in training singers to sing eloquently and act aptly. The restoration of song delivery to its rhetorical roots not only allows the art of eloquent singing to be placed in a broader cultural context but also allows music to take its rightful place beside its sister arts, poetry and oratory. After all, Thomas Campion likened short ayres to quick and good epigrams in poetry, many of them showing as much artifice as larger poems (1613 'To the Reader'). To this end, I am endeavouring to thicken the context of the discussion of early seventeenth-century song, exploring those aspects which music shares with her sister arts as well as those which are unique to music.[7] Hence, the book centres on *elocutio* and *pronunciatio*, drawing on treatises devoted to rhetoric and oration to reconstruct the principles which I believe formed the foundation of both spoken and sung discourse. The techniques of spoken and sung delivery are closely related, as Ascham, Byrd, Vicentino, and Praetorius have noted, and treatises on oration are a natural reservoir for the historically minded modern singer to explore, especially since treatises devoted to music offer so little information on the art of eloquent singing. I will concentrate, therefore, on those techniques which can be transferred easily from one medium to the other. The principles of delivery relating to the voice, written about so extensively in the language arts, pervade every aspect of utterance, and in reconstructing principles of singing from books on rhetoric and oration, the books all educated musicians would have studied in school, we are able to approach the performance of early seventeenth-century lute-song from a broader cultural context. This permits us to create a style of delivery consistent with known tenets of the time.[8]

My arrangement of the material has been inspired by the method of schooling William Kempe prescribed for children (1588 p 233). Kempe suggested young scholars study 'Grammar,' 'Rhetoricall ornaments,' 'pronounciation and gesture,' and 'Logike' in the course of their education. But as my book mainly concerns the techniques of delivery, I have narrowed Kempe's plan to suit my purpose, omitting 'Logike.' *Elocutio* ('Rhetoricall ornaments') is examined first, for, as Quintilian maintains, scholars must understand what they read before they can read well (I pp 146–7). The second part of the book considers *pronunciatio*, focusing on the tangible characteristics of eloquent delivery. My treatment of grammar, which explores the role of punctuation in utterance, appears at the beginning of this section and is followed by discussions of voice (including an examination of that aspect of delivery which is peculiar to music, the art of improvised melodic embellishment) and gesture. The third part concerns the practical application of the early seventeenth-century style of delivery to the songs of John Dowland (1563–1626).

Dowland was one of the best English song-writers ever to have lived, and the skill with which he wed the sister arts of poetry and music was greatly admired in his own time. Both Thomas Campion (writing in 1595) and Richard Barnfield (writing in 1598) paid homage to Dowland, Barnfield praising Dowland's gift as a song-composer with the words 'If music and sweet poetry agree.'⁹ And Henry Peacham the Younger, in a roster of English composers 'inferior to none in the world ... for depth of skill and richnesse of conceipt,' placed 'Master Doctor Douland' at the head of the list (1622 p 103). In fact, Dowland's mastery of affective persuasion through the artful coupling of notes and words remains the aspect of his work which attracts the most attention. Over the past twenty years much has been written about his songs, but only recently has the influence of rhetorical thought on Dowland's compositional procedure been revealed.¹⁰ And it is precisely because of the rhetorical nature of Dowland's music that his songs occupy such a prominent position in this book, for nowhere is the connection between rhetorical delivery and compositional procedure more apparent than in his solo songs. However, the first and second parts of the book do not focus on Dowland's songs exclusively, for I wish to demonstrate that the same sorts of principles of *elocutio* and *pronunciatio* apply to other song-writers as well. But in the third part, an examination of specific songs by Dowland shows how the early seventeenth-century principles discussed in the first two parts may be applied to the lute-song repertoire by modern singers.

Singers today need to become musical orators who arouse passions in listeners through a manner of performance which is designed to approximate the intuitive understanding of delivery that early seventeenth-century singers would have had. The principles behind this style of delivery already were centuries old in Dowland's lifetime. Quintilian relied on the same sorts of techniques that later orators relied on to effect an imitation of man's actions and passions, perfection being achieved only through the combination of words, voice, and gesture: 'And, indeed, since words in themselves count for much and the voice adds a force of its own to the matter of which it speaks, while gesture and motion are full of significance, we may be sure of finding something like perfection when all these qualities are combined' (Quintilian xi pp 246–7).

✤ 1 ELOCUTIO

Happy is hee whose words can move,
Yet sweet Notes help perswasion.
Mixe your words with Musicke then,
That they the more may enter:
(*Campion 1614 no 5*)

Henry Peacham the Younger's direct reference to the 'passionate Aire' as a *prosopopoeia* not only establishes the rhetorical basis of early seventeenth-century lute-song but also hints at the persuasive or affective performing style required by the singer. In rhetoric, *prosopopoeia* involves 'a fayning of any person, when in our speach we represent the person of anie, and make it [him] speake as though he were there present' (Fraunce 1588 f G2r).[1] Or to paraphrase Quintilian (ix pp 390–1) and Peacham the Elder (1577 f O2r–v), the orator personifies the inner thoughts and affections of an absent person, making that person actually seem to appear before the eyes of the hearer. It forms part of a larger group of figures, known generically as *hypotyposis* (*demonstratio* in Latin), which are directed toward lively description or counterfeit representation (Puttenham 1589 p 245). In the case of *prosopopoeia*, the singer feigns the affections of the imaginary person in the poem, bringing forth the ruling passion of that person (often the poet himself). The singer in his musical oration must, then, arouse the passions of the listener through his manner of performance. In order to do this, he must first understand the text and its music in the same way that Elizabethan and Jacobean schoolchildren were taught to understand poetry, orations, etc; that is, he must learn to recognize every figure which adorns the discourse (Kempe 1588 p 233). In other words, the singer must understand *elocutio*, that is, the beautification of the matter through the application of 'apte wordes and picked sentences' (Wilson 1553 p 32). The figures of rhetoric ('apte words and picked sentences') – and those in music – were considered to be important tools for inflaming the mind of the listener as no orator could 'by the waight of his wordes ... perswade his hearers, having no helpe of them [ie the figures]' (Peacham the Elder 1577 f A3r). With figures, 'the Oratour may leade his hearers which way he list, and draw them to what affection he will: he may make them to be angry, to be pleased, to laugh, to weepe, and lament: to love, to abhorre, and loath: to hope, to feare, to covet, to be satisfyed, to envye, to have pittye and compassion: to mervaile, to beleeve, to repent: and briefely to be moved with any affection that shall serve best for his purpose ... [Furthermore, the Oratour may] paynt out any person, deede, or thing, só cunninglye with these couloures, that it shall seeme rather a lyvely Image paynted in tables, then a reporte expressed with the tongue. Fynally, the force of figures is so great, that the strength of apt and eloquent pleading and speaking, consisteth (sayeth Fabius) in these kinde of exornations'[2] (Peacham the Elder 1577 f A3r). Anyone who had received a typical grammar-school education in Elizabethan or Jacobean England would have been highly skilled in recognizing rhetorical devices, and a knowledge of figures was particularly valued as an aid in reading and writing poetry. Henry Peacham the Elder insisted that the utility of 'Fyguratyve Flowers, both of Grammer and Rhetorick ... is so great, that I cannot sufficiently prayse them, and the knowledge of them so necessary, that no man can reade profytably, or understand perfectlye, eyther Poets, Oratours, or the holy Scriptures, without them' (1577 ff A2v–A3r).[3]

Quintilian defined the term figure as a form of speech artfully varied from common usage (IX pp 352–5), and George Puttenham maintained that the 'figure it selfe is a certaine lively or good grace set upon wordes, speaches and sentences to some purpose and not in vaine, giving them ornament or efficacie by many manner of alterations in shape, in sounde, and also in sence, sometime by way of surplusage, sometime by defect, sometime by disorder, or mutation, and also by putting into our speaches more pithe and substance, subtilitie, quicknesse, efficacie or moderation, in this or that sort tuning and tempring them, by amplification, abridgement, opening, closing, enforcing, meekening or otherwise disposing them to the best purpose' (1589 p 171). Figurative speech, then, lifted language from 'the ordinarie habite and manner of our dayly talke and writing' (Puttenham 1589 p 171) to that which was loftier in style. Analogously, figures were employed in music to grace a text and to elevate it from the ordinary to the sublime in order to enhance its style and thus its persuasiveness. Henry Peacham the Younger and Francis Bacon, quoted in the 'Introduction,' make this last point clear, and Henry Peacham the Elder compared the colours of elocution, that is, the figures of grammar and rhetoric, to 'flowers of sundry coullors, a gallant Garland: such as garnish it, as precious pearles, a gorgious Garment: suche as delight the eares, as pleasant reports, repetions, and running poyntes in Musick' (1577 f A3r). The amount of figurative language an orator employed depended upon the style in which he chose to speak: 'the great or mighty' style, 'the smal' style, or 'the lowe' style (Wilson 1553 p 339). In the high style, the orator used great words and vehement figures, whereas in the small or middle style he moderated his 'heat,' using fewer figures. But in the low style, the orator went plainly to work, speaking only in common words (Wilson 1553 p 339).

Peacham the Elder, in following the traditional rhetorical teaching of English rhetoricians such as Richard Sherry (1550) and Thomas Wilson (1553), classified figures as either tropes or schemes. Tropes served to alter the signification of a word or words from the normal meaning to something not proper but quite close (for example, metaphor). Schemes, on the other hand, removed language from the common custom by creating highly artificial patterns of speech (for example, repetitions of all sorts) (Peacham the Elder 1577 ff BIV, EIV).[4] The traditional view of figures was, however, not the only one current in England, for Peacham's contemporary George Puttenham had devised his own system for classifying figures. In discussing exornation, Puttenham found 'ornament Poeticall' to be of two sorts. One, called *enargia*, was to 'satisfie and delight th'eare only by a goodly outward shew set upon the matter with wordes, and speaches smothly and tunably running.' The second, called *energia*, worked inwardly to stir the mind 'by certaine intendments or sence of such wordes and speaches' (1589 p 155). The purpose of some figures, then, simply was to delight the ear. Through these *auricular* devices, the exclusive property of poets, 'not onely the whole body of a tale in a poeme or historie may be made in such sort pleasant and agreable to the eare, but also every clause by it selfe, and every single word carried in a clause, may have their pleasant sweetenesse apart' (p 172). One way of making clauses 'pleasant and agreable to the eare' was to adorn them with the figure *zeugma (adjunctio)* or its opposite *hypozeuxis (disjunctio)* (Puttenham 1589 pp 175–8). *Zeugma* involves making a single word serve more than one clause. If the common servitor appears in the first clause of a series, it is called *prozeugma:*

> Her beautie perst mine eye, her speach mine wofull hart:
> Her presence all the powers of my discourse.

Here the verb 'perst' 'satisfieth both in sence and congruitie all those other clauses that followe him.' Conversely, with *hypozeuxis* the language is adorned by supplying the same word in more than one clause:

> Unto the king she went, and to the king she said,
> Mine owne liege Lord behold thy poore handmaid.

In this example, the words 'to the king' supply both of the first two clauses, beautifying the language with much 'pleasant sweetenesse.'

The purpose of other figures, called *sensable*, was to stir the mind, and these devices belonged to both poets and orators. They gave language efficacy; that is, by altering conceit or sense, they gave language the power to move listeners (pp 171, 188–9). Puttenham provides a particularly potent example in his description of *emphasis*, the figure whose purpose is to 'inforce the sence of any thing by a word of more than ordinary efficacie.' A much more powerful way of stating 'O gratious, courteous and beautifull woman,' he posits, would be to say 'O rare beautie, ô grace, and curtesie' (p 194). Still other figures served both purposes, delighting the ear while stirring the mind, and these Puttenham called '*Sententious or*

Rhetoricall figures.' According to Puttenham, these devices were reserved for the orator alone, because once words and clauses were 'made as well tunable to the eare, as stirring to the minde,' the orator should apply figures designed 'all at once to beautifie and geve sence and sententiousnes to the whole language at large.' These, the most powerful figures, enlarged the entire matter with all sorts of amplifications and allowed the orator to utter and persuade both copiously and vehemently (pp 155, 171–2, 206). Puttenham was, of course, not really stating anything new here, for earlier writers, such as Henry Peacham the Elder, also recognized that certain types of figures were more persuasive than others. This especially applies to Peacham's 'Schemates Rhetoricall' which 'doe fashion a pleasant, sharpe, evident and gallant kinde of speaking, giving unto matters great strength, perspecuitie and grace' (1577 f H4v). Moreover, embodied in the 'Schemates Rhetoricall' were the techniques of amplification, which Peacham particularly valued, because with them the orator 'may easily draw the mindes of his hearers whether he will, and wynde them into what affection he list ... The Oratoure with helpe thereof, eyther breaketh all in peeces, like a thunderbolt, or else by little and little, like the flowing water, creepeth into the mindes of his hearers, and so by a soft and gentle meanes, at last winneth their consent ... the whole strength of apte and eloquent pleading, sayeth Fabius, consisteth in this kinde of exornation' (1577 ff N2v–N3r).

Striking examples of sententious language are found in the figures of repetition. *Symploche (complexio)*, one of the many different forms of word repetition, occurs 'when one and the selfe [same] word doth begin and end many verses in sute' (Puttenham 1589 p 209). This figure, typical of its class, moves and delights the listener with language that is both sweet and pithy. Puttenham's illustration of a man who sportingly complains about his untrustworthy mistress demonstrates the effect:

> Who made me shent for her loves sake?
> > Myne owne mistresse.
> Who would not seeme my part to take[?]
> > Myne owne mistresse.

Thus spoken discourse achieved its greatest persuasiveness, and hence its highest style, when it was adorned with sententious figures which at once both delighted the ear and stirred the mind.

Similarly, musical discourse reached its loftiest and most passionate state when the texts of songs were copiously decorated with sententious figures. It should be, of course, no surprise that songs received the same treatment as poems and orations, for composers were expected to have a knowledge of poetry. In fact, Charles Butler stated that the most powerful musicians were also poets: 'For hee that knoweth bothe [Poesi and Musik], can best fit his Poesi to his own Musik, and his Musik to his own Poesi. And morover hee is enabled to judg of such verses as ar browght unto him, and, for a neede, soomwhat to alter them; that the woords may bee the more consonant to his present vein' (1636 pp 95–6). According to Butler, a knowledge of poetry not only would allow composers to write their own poems but also would allow them to alter the poems of others to suit their purposes. The type of alteration normally made by English composers in the early seventeenth century involved the amplification of the basic structure of the poetry through the addition of figures not present in the poem. Because singing is the musical equivalent of spoken oration, composers embellished texts in order to turn the written poem, which frequently did not contain the style of amplification needed for successful oral persuasion, into a vehicle through which singers, with the help of figures, could move their listeners to specific passions. And, naturally, Elizabethan and Jacobean composers never would have expected poems to contain these kinds of devices, for the sententious figures which Puttenham lists were reserved for orators (1589 pp 171–2; see also Sherry 1550 p 25). Thomas Hobbes, in his translation of Aristotle's *Rhetoric*, explains why writing and speaking were so different (1637 p 118). Written orations, Hobbes maintains, appear flat when spoken. They lack the types of verbal devices, specifically figures of repetition, so necessary for the orator to move his listeners. One could, however, make writing more persuasive simply by adding these figures – repetitions which become amplification in the spoken realm, inflaming and capturing the listeners' minds. Composers added these and other figures to poems in order to enhance the persuasive quality of the affections expressed in the poems, and singers, being skilled in recognizing the purpose of these devices, based their style of delivery on them. Hence, a knowledge of rhetorical structure was prerequisite to eloquent delivery.

The lute-songs of the early seventeenth century represent some of the loftiest and most affective musical orations of the Elizabethan and Jacobean age and frequently take the form of the lover's complaint.[5] Many of them belong either to the great or mighty style, using many vehement exornations (sententious figures) of both language and music to inflame the passions, or to the middle style, distinguishing the song with fewer ornaments. An enormous number of figures are present in lute-songs, but I will limit my discussion of *elocutio*, for the most part, to those rhetorical and musical figures which singers actually.need to make manifest through their style of delivery. Commonly, the amplifications involve reiterations of words or phrases which emphasize the importance of the repeated material. These figures of repetition, the same ones to which Hobbes referred, not only are some of the basic devices with which lute-song composers amplify poems but also are the kinds of sententious figures which Puttenham describes as the most important ones for altering and affecting the ear and the mind of the listener (1589 p 208). Puttenham explains why orators employ these devices: 'And first of all others your figure that worketh by iteration or repetition of one word or clause doth much alter and affect the eare and also the mynde of the hearer, and therefore is counted a very brave figure both with the Poets and rhetoriciens' (1589 p 208). The frequent use of *epizeuxis (subjunctio)*, the immediate restatement of a word or two for greater vehemency (Peacham the Elder 1577 f J3r), embodies a compositional decision to stress and thus elicit in the listener the state of mind associated with that word. Hoskins maintains that this figure is not to be used except in passion (1599 p 126), and Peacham further notes that it 'may serve aptly to express the vehemencie of any affection, whether it be of joy, sorrow, love, hatred, admiration or any such like, in respect of pleasant affections it may be compared to the quaver in Musicke, in respect of sorrow, to a double sigh of the heart, & in respect of anger, to a double stabbe with a weapons point' (1593 pp 47–8).

Various passages exemplify the procedure. At the opening of John

Danyel's song 'Griefe keepe within' (1606 no 9), subtitled 'M^rs. M.E. her Funerall teares for the death of her husband,' the repetition of the word 'griefe' draws attention to and establishes the character of the ruling passion. In the unadorned poem, printed at the end of the song, the first line reads 'Greefe keep within and scorne to shew but teares.' Danyel, however, reiterates the initial word three times, transforming the line from the poetical realm to the world of oration: 'Griefe, Griefe, Griefe, Griefe, keepe within and scorn, to shew but teares.' If this new line had not been intended to have been sung, it would have, to borrow the words of Thomas Hobbes, been 'justly condemned' in writing (1637 p 118). Nevertheless, this type of repetition is permitted in the spoken realm because in discourse repetition becomes amplification. Playwrights often make effective use of the figure. Particularly germane to Danyel's song is a passage from William Shakespeare's *The Tragedie of King Lear* in which Lear mourns for the dead Cordelia, heightening the expression of his grief through *epizeuxis*: 'Thou'lt come no more, Never, never, never, never, never' (1623 v iii, p 309).[6]

Song-writers frequently expand the notion of *epizeuxis* to include not just one or two words but lengthier phrases. This type of repetition is so common that examples of it can be found in the songs of many English composers of the early seventeenth century.[7] John Dowland, for instance, uses the repetition of the phrases 'that nowe lies sleeping' (line 7) of the first verse of 'Weepe you no more sad fountaines' (1603 no 15) and 'while she lies sleeping' (line 7) of the second verse to emphasize the reconciling effect that sleep has on a troubled mind:

> Weepe you no more sad fountaines,
> 　What need you flowe so fast,
> Looke how the snowie mountaines,
> 　Heav'ns sunne doth gently waste.
> But my sunnes heav'nly eyes
> 　View not your weeping,
> 　That nowe lies sleeping
> 　That nowe lies sleeping
> Softly[,] softly[,] now softly lies sleeping.

Sleepe is a reconciling,
    A rest that peace begets:
Doth not the sunne rise smiling,
    When faire at ev'n he sets,
Rest you, then rest sad eyes,
    Melt not in weeping,
    While she lies sleeping
    While she lies sleeping
Softly[,] softly[,] now softly lies sleeping.

Similarly, to continue with the theme of sleep, Thomas Morley repeats the phrase 'sleepe then my eyes' (line 5) in the first two verses of 'Sleepe slumbringe eyes give rest unto my cares' (1600 no 18) to underscore the importance of sleep for banishing sorrow from one's breast. But in the third verse, this sentiment is suddenly reversed when the poet realizes that his eyes are the true partners of unrest. Morley's repetition of 'wake then my eyes' (line 5) heightens the contrast between the verses and emphasizes the poet's conclusion:

Sleepe slumbringe eyes give rest unto my cares,
My cares the Infants of my troubled braine,
My cares surprisde, surprisde with Blacke dispaire
Doth the assention of my hopes restraine.
Sleepe then my eyes, sleepe then my eyes O sleepe
    & take your Reste
To banishe sorrow, to banishe sorrow from
    a free borne Breste.

My freborne brest borne Free to sorrowes Smarte
Brought in subjection by my wandringe Eye
Whose traytrus sighte conceavd that to my harte,
For which I waile, I sob, I sighe, I Dye.
Sleepe then my eyes, sleepe then my eyes
    disturbed of quiet reste,

> To banishe sorrow, to banish sorrow
> From my captive breste.
>
> My captive brest stounge [stung] by these
>   glistringe starres:
> These glistringe starres: the bewty of the skye:
> That bright blacke skye which doth the
>   soone beames baine:
> From Her sweete comforte on my harts sad eye:
> Wake then my eyes, wake then my eyes trewe
>   partners of unreste:
> For Sorrow still, for Sorrow still must harboure
>   in my breste.
>
>> (1600 no 18; although listed in the table of contents, the
>> piece is actually missing in this source; the text is reproduced
>> here from Oxford, Christ Church Library, ms 439 p 1)

In addition to the pervasive use of *epizeuxis*, the song-composers add two other figures of repetition to the poetry they adapt, *anadiplosis (reduplicatio)* and *epanalepsis (resumptio)*. John Dowland employs both of these figures in his setting of the poem 'In darknesse let mee dwell' (Dowland (R) 1610 no 10). Through *anadiplosis*, that is, the repetition of the last word of one phrase at the beginning of the next (Peacham the Elder 1577 f J3r), the lines

> The roofe Dispaire to barre all cheerfull light from mee
> The wals of marble blacke that moistned still shall weepe

become

> The roofe Dispaire to barre all, all cheerfull light
>   from mee
> The wals of marble blacke that moistned, that moistned
>   still shall weepe, still shall weepe.[8]

In connection with *anadiplosis* Henry Peacham the Elder states: 'This exornation doth not onely serve to the pleasantnesse of sound, but also to adde a certaine increase in the second member' (1593 p 47), and John Hoskins comments: 'And as noe man is sicke in thought upon one thinge, but for some vehemency or distresse, Soe in speech there is noe repeticion without importance' (1599 p 126). The device used by Dowland to end the song is known as *epanalepsis*, a sentence that begins and ends with the same word (Peacham the Elder 1593 p 46). Although Peacham warns that there should not be too many members or words between the beginning and the end, Dowland expands this traditional notion of *epanalepsis* and applies the figure to an entire verse. The words 'In darknesse let mee dwell' open and close the song, and Peacham clarifies the intent of this figure: 'Place a word of importance in the beginning of a sentence to be considered, and in the end to be remembred' (1593 p 46).

Not all figures of repetition, however, were added by composers to turn poetry into musical discourse. Some of the sententious figures discussed above, such as *anadiplosis*, as well as other figures, such as *anaphora* (*repetitio*), were part of the poem's original structure. Although the use of *anaphora*, the same word iterated at the beginning of successive sentences (Fraunce 1588 chap 19), is rare among English song-composers, John Dowland does employ the figure in the first verse of 'Al ye, whom love or fortune hath betraid' (1597 no 14):

> Al ye, whom love or fortune hath betraid;
> All ye, that dream of blisse but live in griefe;
> All ye, whose hopes are evermore delaid;
> All ye, whose sighes or sicknesse wants reliefe;
> Lend eares and teares to mee most haplesse man,
> That sings my sorrowes like the dying Swanne.

The figure serves to delight the ear as well as stir the mind of the listener and is the property of both poets and orators. It is at once both *auricular* and *sententious*. Hoskins comments upon the efficacy of *anaphora*: 'This figure beates uppon one thinge to cause the quicker feeling in the audience, & to awake a sleepie or dull person' (1599 p 127). The same duality of function is true of *anadiplosis*. This figure can be found in a number of poems, where it frequently is used as a link to establish the logical connection between two ideas. Morley employs the figure in the first verse of 'Sleepe slumbringe eyes' to draw attention to the ideas associated with the words 'my cares':[9]

> Sleepe slumbringe eyes give rest unto my cares,
> My cares the Infants of my troubled braine.

Other types of rhetorical figures that were woven into the fabric of poems by poets themselves served to amplify the vehemence of the sentiments expressed. Two figures in particular are found in the songs, *auxesis* (*incrementum* or *progressio*) and *synathroismos* (*congeries* or *accumulatio*). *Auxesis* involves ascending by degrees to the top of some matter as 'when we make our saying grow and increase by an orderly placing of our words, making the latter word always exceede the former, in force of signifycation ... In this fygure, order must be dilligently observed, that the stronger may follow the weaker, and the worthyer the lesse worthy' (Peacham the Elder 1577 f Q2v). In other words, the subject is amplified through a continuous and unbroken series of steps in which each new word is stronger than the last. It is, in short, the 'Orators scaling ladder, by which he climeth to the top of high comparison' (Peacham the Elder 1593 p 169). Perhaps the most famous example of this device from the song repertoire is contained in Dowland's 'Come again: sweet love doth now invite' (1597 no 17):

> Come again: sweet love doth now invite,
> Thy graces that refraine,
> To do me due delight,
> To see, to heare, to touch, to kisse, to die,
> With thee againe in sweetest sympathy.

> Come againe that I may cease to mourne,
> Through thy unkind disdaine:

For now left and forlorne,
I sit, I sigh, I weepe, I faint, I die,
In deadly paine and endlesse miserie.

The fourth line of each verse ascends by degrees to the top of the ladder, both verses using the same structural device to intensify the contrasting sentiments of the poem. The first verse speaks of what would be the ideal chain of events and the second of the painful reality of the situation. The beauty of Dowland's figurative language is that both ladders reach their climax with the word 'die,' the first verse using the word euphemistically and the second verse using it literally. Dowland further reinforces the antithetical nature of the poem by summarizing the contrasting sentiments of the two verses in the last words of each stanza: 'sweetest sympathy' versus 'endlesse miserie.'[10]

Similar passages are found in other songs. Thomas Morley, for example, employs the same sort of ladder in the second verse of 'Sleepe slumbringe eyes' (line 4):

My freborne brest borne Free to sorrowes Smarte
Brought in subjection by my wandringe Eye
Whose traytrus sighte conceaved that to my harte,
For which I waile, I sob, I sighe, I Dye.
Sleepe then my eyes, disturbed of quiet reste,
To banishe sorrow From my captive breste.

And Philip Rosseter uses the device to lead the anguish of the speaker's torments from the earthly realm to the celestial in the first verse of 'No grave for woe' (line 4):[11]

No grave for woe, yet earth my watrie teares devoures,
Sighes want ayre, and burnt desires kind pitties showres,
Stars hold their fatal course my joyes preventing,
The earth, the sea, the aire, the fire, the heav'ns vow my tormenting.
(1601 no 3)

John Danyel, however, increases the complexity of his figurative language by coupling *auxesis* with *epimone (versus intercalaris)*, the regular repetition of one phrase at equal distance because that phrase 'beareth the whole burden of the song' (Puttenham 1589 p 233), to continually re-emphasize the depth of sorrow Mrs. M.E. shows with her 'Funerall teares for the death of her husband' (last line of each verse):

The first part.

> Greefe keep within and scorne to shew but teares,
> Since Joy can weepe as well as thou:
> Disdaine to sigh for so can slender cares,
>   Which but from Idle causes grow.
> Doe not looke forth unlesse thou didst know how
> To looke with thine owne face, and as thou art,
> And onely let my hart,
> That knowes more reason why,
> Pyne, fret, consume, swell, burst and dye.

The second part.

> Drop not myne eyes nor Trickle downe so fast,
> For so you could doe oft before,
> In our sad farewells and sweet meetings past,
> And shall his death now have no more?
> Can niggard sorrow yeld no other store:
> To shew the plentie of afflictions smart,
> Then onely thou poore hart,
> That knowst more reason why,
> Pyne, Fret, Consume, Swell, Burst and Dye.

The third part.

> Have all our passions certaine proper vents,
> And sorow none that is her owne?
> But she must borow others complements,
> To make her inward feelings knowne?
> Are Joyes delights and deathes compassion showne,

With one lyke face and one lamenting part?
Then onely thou poore hart
That know'st more reason why,
Pine, Fret, Consume, Swell, Burst, and Dye.

Synathroismos, on the other hand, entails a different type of amplification, one which involves 'a multiplication or heaping togeather of
manye wordes, sygnifyinge dyvers thinges of like nature' (Peacham the
Elder 1577 f Q2r). John Dowland accumulates many words of the same
meaning in 'If fluds of teares' (1600 no 11) in order to reach the same sort
of climax that one could achieve through *auxesis*, the main difference
being that in *synathroismos* the effect is attained not through a series of
graduated steps but by piling up words (Peacham the Elder 1593 p 169)
(lines 5 and 6):

If fluds of teares could cleanse my follies past,
And smoakes of sighes might sacrifice for sinne,
If groning cries might salve my fault at last,
Or endles mone, for error pardon win,
Then would I cry, weepe, sigh, and ever mone,
Mine errors, fault[s], sins, follies past and gone.

And Robert Jones heaps together various words to emphasize the folly of
youths who make love a god only to be bound by marriage (line 3):

Fond wanton youths make love a God,
Which after proveth ages rod,
Their youth, their time, their wit, their arte,
They spend in seeking of their smarte,
    And which of follies is the chiefe,
    They wooe their woe, they wedde their griefe.
        (1600 no 2, first verse)

Composers were not content, however, merely to decorate the poetry
with figures, for although the exornations which they added to the texts

of songs enhanced the persuasiveness of the poetry, the passionate appeal
of that sententious language could be heightened even more by introduc-
ing musical figures to parallel poetic devices. In fact, the ability to com-
bine words and music in this way lies at the heart of song composition,
and Thomas Campion captured the essence of the composer's task so
perfectly in the passage quoted at the beginning of this section:

> Happy is hee whose words can move,
>> Yet sweet Notes help perswasion.
> Mix your words with Musicke then,
>> That they the more may enter.
>> (1614 no 5)

Throughout the entire corpus of early seventeenth-century English lute-
song, figures of melodic repetition frequently coincide with textual
figures, and *palillogia*, *synonymia*, *climax*, and *gradatio*, as well as *articulus*,[12]
are clearly favoured for setting textual *epizeuxis* and *auxesis*.

  Palillogia, the repetition of a melodic fragment at the same pitch
(Bartel 1985 pp 222–4), occurs in John Dowland's 'Farewell too faire'
(1603 no 1) for the immediate reiteration of single words (Ex 1.1a) and in
his setting of Fulke Greville's 'Who ever thinks or hopes of love' (1597
no 2) for the repetition of short phrases (Ex 1.1b).

Ex 1.1 (a) 'Farewell too faire'

se-   cre- sie,   fare-well,   fare-well.

(b) 'Who ever thinks or hopes of love'

The rhetorical parallel of this musical device explains its effect. In the language arts, this figure serves to add weight to the idea expressed in the text by emphasizing a particular aspect of its meaning, as 'when the word repeated hath another signification' (Peacham the Elder 1577 f J2v [Diaphora]). Peacham supplies the following example: 'What man is there living, that would not have pitied that case if he had bene a man. In the latter place man signifieth humanitie, or the pittifull affection that is in man' (f J2v). This notion of repetition drawing attention to another meaning associated with the repeated word lies at the heart of the musical device, for an exact repetition of a melodic fragment gives new significance to the repeated material. And when musical devices are coupled with rhetorical figures, the vehemency of persuasion is enhanced in a way that would have been impossible for either music or language to achieve on their own. Charles Butler, in discussing the repetition of points ('a Point is a certain number and order of observable Notes in any one Parte, iterated in the same or in divers Partes' [1636 p 71]), stresses that melodic repetition increases the listener's understanding of the subject matter of the poem: 'If the Point[']s Ditti bee not apprehended at the first; yet, in the iterating thereof, it [the Ditti] may. Such Repetes shoolde bee Emphatical [that is, should accompany important words or phrases], importing soom special matter: and which, in Divine uses, may help bothe to excite and to expres due zele and Devotion' (1636 p 97). By pairing musical *palillogia* with textual *epizeuxis* in 'Farewell too faire' and 'Who ever thinks or hopes of love,' Dowland makes the passages both *auricular* and *sententious*, and this simultaneously delights the ear and affects the mind of the listener.

At other times, composers set the restatement of short phrases and single words by means of *synonymia*, the repetition of a melodic fragment at a different pitch level (but not one step higher or lower).[13] The rhetorical connotations of this term also help to illuminate the musical function of the figure. In the language arts, *synonymia* specifies a figure designed to make the sense stronger and more obvious by using words which differ from the preceding ones in form or sound but which mean the same (Sherry 1550 p 49, Peacham the Elder 1577 f P4r, Puttenham 1589 p 223). George Puttenham (1589 p 223) provides an example:

> What is become of that beautifull face,
> Those lovely lookes, that favour amiable,
> Those sweete features, and visage full of grace,
> That countenance which is alonly able
> To kill and cure?

> Ye see that all these words, face, lookes, favour, features, visage, countenance, are in sence all but one. Which store, neverthelesse, doeth much beautifie and inlarge the matter.

The parallel between the musical figure and its rhetorical antecedent is obvious. In music, the repetition of a melodic fragment at another pitch level may be viewed as using notes which mean the same (because the intervallic integrity of the fragment is maintained) but sound different (because the fragment actually is stated on new notes).

In the first verse of 'Behold a wonder here' (1603 no 3), John Dowland reiterates the word 'hundred' (line 3 below) to stress the length of time that love had been blind. His decision to utilize the musical figure *synonymia* at this point draws further attention to the word, and his melodic design duplicates the type of inflection that one might have employed when speaking the line (Ex 1.2):

> Behold a wonder here
> Love hath receiv'd his sight
> Which manie hundred yeares,
> Hath not beheld the light.

Ex 1.2 'Behold a wonder here'

Repeated phrases similarly are set to *synonymia*, and this frequently provides the *auricular* pleasure that was so much a part of sententious language. Such is the case with Francis Pilkington's setting of Thomas Watson's poem 'With fragrant flowers we strew the way' (1605 no 20). The refrain of this song reads 'O gracious King, of second Troy, accept of our unfained joy,' and Pilkington chose to highlight the most important words in the refrain 'O gracious King,' the words which praise James I,[14] through *synonymia* (Ex 1.3).

Interestingly, Pilkington arranges his restatements of the melodic fragment in a way that is similar to John Hoskins' description of another device which I discussed earlier, the rhetorical figure *auxesis*. In fact, Hoskins' comments exactly parallel Pilkington's use of musical *synonymia*: '[To] make the matter seeme the higher advaunced, sometimes [the figure] descends the lower; it is a bad grace in dancing either to shrinke much in, or sincke farr downe, that you may rise the higher caper, But it is an ornament in speech, to begin att the lowest that you the better

aspire to the height of amplyficacion' (1599 p 140). Pilkington states the
melodic idea and then descends 'the lower' so that the textual *epizeuxis*
may rise to the height of amplification. Once again, figurative language is
made even more persuasive through the combination of musical and
rhetorical devices.

Ex 1.3 'With fragrant flowers we strew the way'

When the quasi-ladder effect Pilkington has created in this passage is
arranged in a stepwise progression, the musical figure is known as *climax
(gradatio)* (Bartel 1985 pp 122–7).[15] Thomas Wilson defines the figure in
rhetoric as one in which 'the worde, whiche endeth the sentence goyng
before, doeth begin the nexte.' His example demonstrates the structure of
the device: 'Labour getteth learnyng, learnyng getteth fame, fame getteth
honour, honour getteth blesse for ever' (1553 pp 405–6). George
Puttenham expands the notion of this figure, characterizing it as one in
which 'after the first steppe all the rest proceede by double the space, and
so in our speach one word proceedes double to the first that was spoken,
and goeth as it were by strides or paces' (1589 p 217). John Hoskins also
comments on the vehement effect of this figure and states that with *cli-*

max we are led by degrees in which the last word is made a step to further meaning (1599 p 126), and Peacham the Elder reminds the orator that the figure usually consists of three or four degrees and should end with a clause of importance (1593 pp 133–4). Comparisons of the figure to stairs (Wilson 1553 p 405), or degrees (Peacham the Elder 1577 f Q3r), or steps (Hoskins 1599 p 126), or ladders (Puttenham 1589 p 217) are common, and it is this aspect of the figure which creates two musical figures from one rhetorical figure. Both the rhetorical figure and its musical counter-parts serve the same purpose; that is, through carefully graduated increments, they increase the vehemence of the passions expressed in the text. And like Pilkington's use of *synonymia* in 'With fragrant flowers we strew the way,' musical *climax/gradatio* usually begins at the lowest point and ascends to the top, creating in music the same effect that Hoskins attributes to rhetorical *auxesis*. Thomas Morley employs musical *climax* in 'I saw my Ladye weeping' (1600 no 5) to emphasize the fairness and per-fection of his lady's eyes into which sorrow was so proud to have crept (Ex 1.4):

> I saw my Ladye weeping,
> And sorrowe proud to bee advaunced so,
> In those fayre eyes Where all perfection kept
> Her face was full of woe,
> But such a woe, Beeleeve mee as winnes mennes heartes,
> Then myrth can doo with her intising partes.

Ex 1.4 'I saw my Ladye weeping'

And Thomas Ford takes full advantage of the technique to heighten the desperation of the speaker in 'Faire, sweet, cruell' (1607 no 7). The repetition of the words 'tarrie then' (line 5) leads to the exclamation 'Oh tarrie,' and the use of *climax* to set 'tarrie then, tarrie then' allows the speaker to ascend by degrees to the emotional outburst that precedes his insistence that his lady take him with her (Ex 1.5):

> Faire, sweet cruell, why doest thou flie mee, why dost
>   thou flie me,
> Go not, goe not, oh goe not from thy deerest,
> Though thou doest hasten I am nie thee
> When thou see'mst farre then am I neerest,
>   Tarrie then Tarrie then Oh tarrie,
>   Oh tarrie then and take me with you.

Ex 1.5 'Faire, sweet, cruell'

In musical *gradatio*, however, a true ladder is formed. The purest form of this figure, that is, the one which parallels the rhetorical definition the most closely, is found in the song repertoire in settings of both textual

epizeuxis and textual *auxesis*. The steps in the graduated climb from earth
to heaven *(auxesis)* in Rosseter's 'No grave for woe' (1601 no 3) are linked
one to another, with the last note of one step becoming the first note of
the next (Ex 1.6a). And John Dowland employs the same type of ladder to
heighten the torturous ascent from tears, to sighs, to groans and from
fear, to grief, to pain in the third and fourth verses of 'Flow my teares'
(1600 no 2) (Ex 1.6b).

Ex 1.6 (a) 'No grave for woe' (b) 'Flow my teares'

But Thomas Campion uses this pure form of musical *gradatio* to set textual *epizeuxis* in 'Mistris since you so much desire' (1601 no 16). His
choice of words to depict through *gradatio* is an obvious one, and
Campion musically portrays each step of the ladder as the speaker's lady
looks 'but a little higher' for the place of Cupid's fire (Ex 1.7):

> Mistris since you so much desire,
> To know the place of Cupids fire,
> In your faire shrine that flame doth rest,

Yet never harbourd in your brest,
It bides not in your lips so sweete
Nor where the rose and lillies meete,
    But a little higher,
There there, O there lies Cupids fire.

Ex 1.7 'Mistris since you so much desire'

However, another form of musical *gradatio*, one in which the steps of the ladder are not linked to one another but are steps in the sense that each one is a single degree higher in the musical scale, was used by song-composers. Campion, once again, chooses the most obvious words to set to this latter form of rising ladder. In 'Sweet exclude mee not' (1613/2 no 11), the phrase 'yet a little more' receives the same sort of literal treatment as 'but a little higher' (Ex 1.8).

One can, of course, traverse a ladder in two directions, and composers did not miss the opportunity to use descending ladders to depict the sense of the poetry. Francis Pilkington's setting of Campion's poem 'Now let her change and spare not' (1605 no 8) employs downward *gradatio* for the words 'But she is gon' (line 5), Pilkington imposing an interpretation on

Ex 1.8 'Sweet exclude mee not'

the poem which reflects, perhaps, the sinking realization that the woman who has proved so false is actually gone (Ex 1.9):

> Now let her change and spare not,
> Since she proves false I care not,
> Fained love so bewitched my delight,
> That still I doated on her sight,
> But she is gon, New desires imbracing,
> And my deserts disgracing.

Ex 1.9 'Now let her change and spare not'

Gradatio also is used to set another sort of repetition, not the repetition of the same word as in *epizeuxis*, but the kind Abraham Fraunce describes as the repetition of like sounds. Fraunce defines this rhetorical figure, *paronomasia (allusio)*, as one in which 'a word is changed in signification by changing of a letter or sillable' (1588 chap 24). Through it, words that are similar in sound but different in meaning are juxtaposed, and this is one of the ways of creating the utmost grace in poetry, especially if it is not used too often (Peacham the Elder 1593 p 56). Robert Jones adorns all three verses of 'Whither runneth my sweet hart' (1601 no 12) with this device and embeds the figure within either musical *gradatio* or *climax* (Ex 1.10).

Ex 1.10 'Whither runneth my sweet hart'

On numerous occasions, the figurative language just discussed was made even more sententious by combining textual *epizeuxis* and musical *climax/gradatio* with *articulus (brachylogia)*. In rhetoric, *articulus* refers to the separation of 'words & clauses one from another, either by distinguishing the sound [with commas], or by separating the sense' (Peacham the Elder 1593 p 56). It serves to express any vehement affection, and Peacham the Elder states that 'in peaceable and quiet causes it may be compared to a sembreefe in Musicke, but in causes of perturbation and hast, it may be likened to thicke & violent strokes' (1593 p 57). Peacham's equation of *articulus* to the semibreve suggests that semibreves, at least in 'peaceable and quiet causes,' should be separated from one another by some sort of an articulation. Indeed, certain composers seem to concur with Peacham's observation, for both John Danyel and Robert Jones compose rests into their vocal lines to separate semibreves from other notes when their songs begin with repetitions of the word grief (Ex 1.11).

Ex 1.11 (a) 'Griefe keepe within' (Danyel 1606 no 9)
(b) 'Griefe of my best loves absenting' (Jones 1609 no 14)

(a)

Griefe,   Griefe,   Griefe,   Griefe,   keepe with-in

(b)

Griefe,   griefe of my   best

At other times, *articulus* is combined with musical *gradatio* in order to further strengthen the affective power of textual *epizeuxis*. By separating the restatements of a melodic fragment, thereby paralleling commas in the text, a composer can draw further attention to the affection associated with the repeated word. Robert Jones achieves this effect most persuasively in 'My love bound me with a kisse' (1601 no 2). He momentarily suspends the frivolous nature of the text with a mock-serious exclamatory outburst of 'Alas' (line 5) set to a rising *gradatio* of falling thirds, the increasing vehemence of each step of the ladder being accentuated by rests (Ex 1.12):

> My love bound me with a kisse
> That I should no longer stay
> When I felt so sweete a blisse,

I had lesse power to part away,
Alas that women doth not know
Kisses makes men loath to goe.

Ex 1.12 'My love bound me with a kisse'

In addition to heightening the passionate appeal of textual *epizeuxis*, *articulus* plays an important role in *synathroismos*, and composers some-times set the accumulated words to the longer note values of the semi-breve or minim. This approach parallels Peacham the Elder's description of the device and affords performers the opportunity to clearly detach each word from the rest of the series, thus enabling the listener to momentarily reflect upon every word in the figure. Dowland makes full use of the rhetorical connotations of semibreves, and by extension minims in slower tempos, to increase the climactic effect of the words 'But thinks sighes, teares, vowes, praiers, and sacrifices' in 'Times eldest sonne' (1600 no 6) (Ex 1.13a) and the words 'Deare, sweet, faire, wise' in 'Deare, if you change' (1597 no 7) (Ex 1.13b).

Ex 1.13 (a) 'Times eldest sonne'

(b) 'Deare, if you change'

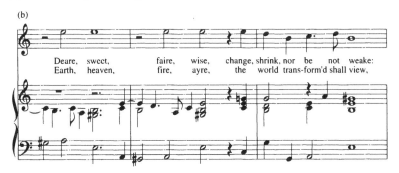

The rhetorical artifice present in the songs of the early seventeenth century does more than control much of the melodic structure, however; it influences the very character of the *concentus*, that is, the vertical combination of notes sounding together. In many songs, especially those dealing with sorrow, grief, sadness, etc, musical figures involving dissonant elements help to establish the ruling passion and to enhance the impact of the text. In particular, certain composers exploit non-harmonic relations (the *mi-fa* clash of the false relation or other dissonances between parts [Bartel 1985 pp 231–3]), or in musical-rhetorical terms *parrhesia (licentia)* to express the passions of sorrow and grief. The parallel between music and the language arts is clarified by the rhetorical definition of the figure: the use of pungent language to reprehend the hearers for some fault (*Rhetorica* IV pp 348–55). Abraham Fraunce adds the idea that this figure is a type of exclamation in which one speaks boldly and confidently (1588 chap 27).[16] John Danyel's three-part song 'Griefe keepe within' (1606 no 9) is a virtual thesaurus of figures of dissonance both within the lute accompaniment itself and between the lute and voice parts. The highly dissonant nature of the music constantly reminds us of the grief and sorrow Mrs. M.E. feels after the death of her husband. In many passages of the song, Danyel combines musical figures to generate a web of devices that pervades the entire texture. The music for the words 'Since Joy can weepe as well as thou' (Ex 1.14) not only incorporates *gradatio* in the voice part but also includes *parrhesia* (false relations within the voice part itself between C and C♯ as well as direct dissonance between the voice and the lute, C♯/F). In addition to these two figures, the excerpt contains an unprepared dissonance created by the leap from a consonant note (B in the voice part) to a dissonant one (D), or *heterolepsis* (Bartel 1985 pp 184–6).

Ex 1.14 'Griefe keepe within'

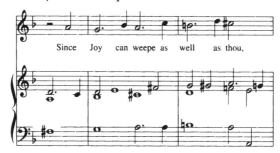

Other passages intensify the rhetorical persuasion using various techniques. For the words 'Griefe, keepe within,' Danyel chose to couple *syncope* (a suspension [Bartel 1985 pp 262–9]) with *syncopatio catachrestica* (an irregular resolution of a suspension [Bernhard p 77; trans Hilse 1973 pp 102–3]) (Ex 1.15). The suspended A in the voice part of this example resolves not to a consonant note but to a dissonant one, and this helps to maintain tension in the vertical sonority.

Ex 1.15 'Griefe keepe within'

In the second part of the song, Danyel employs *mutatio toni*, an abrupt change in *concentus* for expressive purposes (Bartel 1985 pp 216–19), to characterize through modal instability the distress which continued suffering causes (Ex 1.16, especially the latter portion).

Ex 1.16 'Griefe keepe within'

Similar in effect to these figures is *pathopoeia (imaginatio)*. This is the generic term, also used by *musica poetica* theorists to designate chromaticism (Bartel 1985 pp 234–6), for two categories of rhetorical devices that move the minds of listeners to indignation, anger, fear, envy, hatred, hope, gladness, mirth, laughter, sorrow, or sadness. The first type is called imagination and embraces 'sharp figures' that stir the sorts of vehement affections that one finds in tragedy, that is, matters which are great, cruel, horrible, marvellous, pleasant, etc. The second type is called commiseration through which the orator brings his listeners to tears or moves them to pity or forgiveness (Sherry 1550 p 68 and Peacham the Elder 1577 f P3r). In music, composers often set certain of these vehement affections to rising or falling chromatic lines, using chromaticism to underline the torment of words such as woe, bitter grief, sorrow, mists and darkness, and tears[17] (see Ex 1.17 for one such setting by Thomas Ford).

Ex 1.17 'Goe passions to the cruell faire' (Ford 1607 no 5)

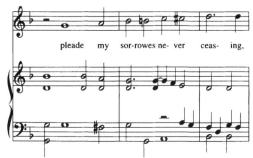

Through the discussions of *pathopoeia* which survive from the period, not only are we alerted to the rhetorical nature of chromaticism in the song repertoire but also we discover which rhetorical figures Peacham the Elder considers to be the most suitable for stirring the vehement affections he describes. At the head of Peacham's list of 'sharp figures,' we find *ecphonesis (exclamatio)*, a device regularly employed in song poetry, which Peacham characterizes as follows: 'when through affection either of anger, sorrow, gladnesse, marveyling, feare, or any such lyke, we breake out in voyce with an exclamation, & outcry to express the passions of our minde, after this manner. O lamentable estate, O cursed misery, O wicked impudency, O joy imcomparable, O rare and singuler bewty' (1577 f κ4r). His description of the figure is reinforced by his compatriot George Puttenham who advises that such outcries are embodied in all words that show extreme passion (1589 p 221). And Abraham Fraunce gives us a list of the range of affections the figure covers: wonder and admiration, despair, wishing, indignation, derision, protestation or obtestation, grief and misery, pity and commiseration, and cursing (1588 chap 27). Peacham the Elder cautions, however, that *ecphonesis* should not be used too often lest it become odious (1593 p 63). Most of the sentences containing these emotional outbursts, as illustrated by Peacham's examples given above, begin with an exclamatory 'O!' or 'Alas!'.[18] Composers usually set this opening expletive to the longer notes of the semibreve, the dotted minim, or the minim, Dowland favouring the dotted minim or semibreve and other composers preferring the minim. These longer notes, particularly dotted minims and semibreves, draw attention to the exclamatory interjection and allow singers time to colour the note dynamically (Ex 1.18).[19]

Ex 1.18 'Sweet stay a while' (Dowland 1612 no 2)

Related to *pathopoeia* and *ecphonesis*, with their vivid depiction of vehement affections, is another figure, the music theorist's *hypotyposis (demonstratio)*, which acts as a generic term for any musical device that serves to illustrate the text in a literal fashion (Bartel 1985 pp 196–8). Examples of this sort of pictorial representation are common, and in the song repertoire composers frequently set words referring to rising and height or sinking and lowness to melodies moving either up *(anabasis)* or down *(catabasis)* (Bartel 1985 pp 84–5, 115–16). Sighs are depicted by rests, and words that are also terms for musical ornaments, such as relish, occasionally are set to written-out forms of the embellishments.[20] Robert Jones' depiction of the words 'now up now downe' typifies the approach to this kind of text setting (Ex 1.19).

Ex 1.19 'When love on time' (Jones 1600 no 9)

But composers can, of course, vividly portray poetry in much subtler ways, and John Dowland perfectly blends music and rhetoric at the close of 'In darknesse let mee dwell' (Dowland (R) 1610 no 10). In rhetorical delivery, the orator's emotional state can be demonstrated most vehemently through a speech that is terminated without a word of explanation, as when the orator's sorrow is too great to continue (Peacham the Elder 1577 f N1v). Dowland brilliantly constructs 'In darknesse let mee dwell' to produce this effect (Ex 1.20). Textual and musical *epanalepsis* concludes the song, and the melody fashioned by Dowland for this purpose ends unexpectedly with a remarkably short resolution of the prolonged *syncope*.[21] This hasty abandonment of the last note of the song creates the musical counterpart of *aposiopesis*, the rhetorical figure denoting abrupt terminations.

Ex 1.20 'In darknesse let mee dwell'

Up to this point, I have concentrated on passages from the songs in which composers chose to augment the persuasive qualities of rhetorical figures in the text with musical figures. But not every textual figure was reflected in the music, especially when a figure, such as *auxesis*, appears in a second or third verse but not in the first. In Thomas Morley's 'Sleepe slumbringe eyes' (1600 no 18), for example, the textual *auxesis* discussed earlier is contained in the second verse alone. Undoubtedly, few composers would have missed the opportunity for setting this figure to musical *gradatio*, but since Morley obviously conceived his music in terms of the first verse, he was unable to provide special musical treatment for figures which appeared in later verses. His song, then, lends support to my belief that many composers wrote their music to suit the first verse and rarely worried about the appropriateness of that music for subsequent verses. And one certainly observes this same phenomenon in many other strophic songs. Textual figures in first verses frequently receive detailed musical figuration, so detailed in fact that later verses often fit the music most imperfectly. In John Dowland's 'O sweet woods' (1600 no 10), the seventh line of the first verse reads 'To birds, to trees, to earth, impart I this,' and Dowland appropriately parallels the textual *articulus* with rests in the melody. This melody is, however, most unsuitable for the remaining three verses. The corresponding lines in these verses are conceived as longer, continuous phrases, and the forward motion of these lines is interrupted by the halting effect of the rests in Dowland's melody (Ex 1.21).[22]

Ex 1.21 'O sweet woods'

A notable exception to this practice is the work of Thomas Campion. In some of his songs, Campion conceived his poetry and music in such a way that in all verses, to borrow Campion's frequently quoted phrase, the words and notes could be coupled lovingly together (1613/1 'To the Reader'). In 'Author of light' (1613/1 no 1), for example, the music works as well for the second verse as it does for the first (Ex 1.22).

Ex 1.22 'Author of light'

A possible explanation for this difference between Campion and his compatriots is that Campion set his own poetry to music whereas, if Robert Jones' statement regarding his willingness 'to embrace the conceits of such gentlemen as were earnest to have me apparell these [ie, their] ditties for them' (1600 'To the Reader') is typical, other composers often set poems written by anonymous courtiers. Thus, composers were not always afforded the luxury of conceiving their poetry and music simultaneously.

Interestingly, the songbooks also contain works in which the music seems to have been composed with the second verse in mind instead of the first – exactly the opposite situation to that found in 'O sweet woods.' In Dowland's setting of the poem 'The lowest trees have tops' (1603 no 19), ascribed to Sir Edward Dyer,[23] the music for the final line of each verse most clearly was inspired by the second verse and not the first (Ex 1.23). The rising *gradatio* perfectly suits the words 'They heare, and see, and sigh' but the corresponding words in the first verse 'and love is love in beggers' would not have suggested, I believe, the *gradatio* figure to early seventeenth-century composers.

Ex 1.23 'The lowest trees have tops'

However, the songs do contain a number of musical figures for which no parallel textual devices exist, and although rhetoric and music were sister arts in late Elizabethan and Jacobean England, the presence of these figures reminds us that some musical devices were *auricular* rather than *sententious*. In other words, composers did not always couple musical and rhetorical figures every time the opportunity arose. John Dowland, for instance, occasionally employs musical *climax* not to underscore textual *epizeuxis*, one of the most common uses of *climax*, but simply to set the first two lines of 'When others sings Venite exultemus' (1600 no 8) to the same musical phrase repeated one step higher (Ex 1.24).[24]

Ex 1.24 'When others sings Venite exultemus'

And just as musical figures are used for their own sake, as in Ex 1.24, textual devices are present without support from their musical counterparts. *Epizeuxis*, for example, receives no further help in Dowland's 'I saw my Lady weepe' (1600 no 1) (Ex 1.25), and *anaphora*, an obvious choice I would have thought for strengthening the persuasiveness of the iterated words through the repetition of the same melodic fragment, was overlooked in his 'Al ye, whom love or fortune hath betraid' (1597 no 14).

Ex 1.25 'I saw my Lady weepe'

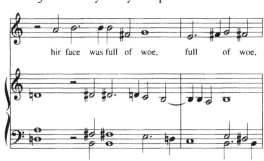

Nonetheless, to a greater or lesser degree (perhaps corresponding to higher or lower styles), the vast majority of songs from this period do 'fit the Note to the Word' (Robert Jones 1600 'To the Reader'), enjoying a coupling of music and rhetoric worthy of Campion's remarks, quoted at the outset, which act as a proposition for this whole section:[25]

> Happy is hee whose words can move,
>   Yet sweet Notes help perswasion.
> Mixe your words with Musicke then,
>   That they the more may enter.
>   (1614 no 5)

The discussion of these songs through rhetorical concepts and terminology – the precepts most relevant to the vocal music of this period – helps modern musicians not accustomed to the principles of rhetoric to acquire the necessary tools for identifying the significance of musical procedures that they might otherwise pass over. Moreover, a knowledge of the musical-rhetorical structure of the song repertoire provides modern singers with the same skills seventeenth-century singers would have possessed, and the ability to recognize technical devices enables singers to construct an appropriate framework within which to place their intuitive emotional responses to the songs. Once singers understand the purpose of figures, they are in a position to generate in listeners those passions that are present in the text. In this regard, performers would do well to bear in mind the words of Henry Peacham the Elder that I quoted earlier: 'The force of figures is so great, that the strength of apt and eloquent pleading and speaking, consisteth (sayeth Fabius) in these kinde of exornations' (1577 f A3r). Thus, we must use our knowledge of rhetorical devices to help us inflame and capture the minds and hearts of our listeners. The ensuing discussion of the methods for delivering figurative language will familiarize singers with the techniques of voice and gesture that form the basis of persuasive singing.

2 PRONUNCIATIO

So sweet is thy discourse:
please the Eye, charm the Ear, and move the Passions
(Campion 1618/4 no 6/Le Faucheur 1657 p 37)

The main purpose of early seventeenth-century song delivery was to persuade listeners using a style of utterance that had two principal parts – singing eloquently and acting aptly.[1] These two parts, voice and gesture, are the external signs of internal passions, and singers make their internal passions manifest by appealing to the ears and the eyes of the listener, the two sensory organs through which all affections penetrate the soul (Quintilian XI pp 248–51). But in order to successfully capture the minds of listeners, the singer must discover what passions are contained in the song and use the textual and musical figures with which the song already has been beautified to help make the imaginary person in the poem actually seem to appear before the listeners. The style of utterance, therefore, must suit the emotions of the poem perfectly, for persuasive delivery was the fundamental goal of spoken and musical oration.

Thomas Wilson defined *pronunciatio* as 'an apte orderinge bothe of the voyce, countenaunce, and all the whole bodye, accordynge to the worthines of suche woordes and mater as by speache are declared' (1553 p 431). It was, as mentioned earlier, the most important part of rhetoric in late sixteenth- and early seventeenth-century England, and the mastery of utterance was one of the main functions of education in the language arts.

Training in delivery, educators declared, should begin early, John Brinsley insisting that in grammar schools pronunciation should be taught in the lowest forms (1622 p 55). Brinsley also recommended that students apply the same principles of delivery to both poetry and prose: 'So in all Poetry, for the pronuntiation, it is to be uttered as prose; observing distinctions and the nature of the matter; not to bee tuned foolishly or childishly after the manner of scanning a Verse as the use of some is' (1612 p 213). Moreover, prospective orators needed to practise, for both nature and art require regular exercise to transform students into potent persuaders (Wright 1604 p 183). Pupils should select good masters with whom to study and should always bear in mind that the '*Rules of this Art ... are far more magnificent in Practice than in Praecept*' (Le Faucheur 1657 pp 207–8).[2] The road to excellence, then as now, must have been arduous, for one of the basic methods of perfecting delivery was to repeat a sentence over and over until one could pronounce it 'according to *Art*' (Le Faucheur 1657 p 214). It was, in fact, *prosopopoeias*, exclamations, and the like that Elizabethan and Jacobean schoolchildren were encouraged to study when practising the imitation of affections,[3] and these texts demanded a passionate manner of declamation, speakers using both voice and gesture to bring forth the emotions of the text. Thomas Wright underscored the importance of employing voice and gesture to imitate passions: 'Furthermore, the passion passeth not only thorow the eyes, but also pierceth the eare, and thereby the heart; for a flexible and plyable voyce, accommodated in manner correspondent to the matter whereof a person intreateth, conveyeth the passion most aptly, pathetically, & almost harmonically, & every accent, exclamation, admiration, increpation, indignation, commiseration, abhomination, exanimation, exultation, fitly (that is, distinctly, at time and place, with gesture correspondent, and flexibilitie of voice proportionate) delivered, is either a flash of fire to incense a passion, or a bason of water to quench a passion incensed' (1604 p 175). Thus the affections of listeners are moved through two closely related channels – the subject matter itself, which is perceived by the ears, and the action of the person concerned, which is seen with the eyes (Wilson 1553 p 266).

But, of course, these channels work effectively to stir the minds of others only when the orator/singer first is moved by the passions in the text himself, for as Thomas Wright asserted, 'it is almost impossible for an Orator to stirre up a Passion in his auditors, except he bee first affected with the same passion himselfe' (1604 p 172). In the same vein, Thomas Wilson, writing under the heading 'Heate, causeth heate,' declared that 'nothyng kyndeleth soner then fire. And therefore a fierie stomack, causeth evermore a fierie tongue. And he that is heated with zeale and godlinesse, shall set other on fire with like affeccion' (1553 p 273). He even suggested that in representing grief the orator actually should weep: 'Again, nothyng moysteth soner then water. Therefore a wepyng iye causeth muche moysture, and provoketh teares. Neither is it any mervaile: for suche men bothe in their countenaunce, tongue, iyes, gesture, and in all their body els, declare an outwarde grief, and with wordes so vehemently and unfeinedly, settes it forward, that thei will force a man to be sory with them, and take part with their teares, even against his will' (pp 273–4). There is, of course, nothing new in Wilson's suggestion. In the first century AD, Quintilian admitted that he often was moved to tears when speaking: 'I have frequently been so much moved while speaking, that I have not merely been wrought upon to tears, but have turned pale and shown all the symptons of genuine grief' (vi pp 438–9). But one should not dwell too long in such affections, for 'though a vehement talke maie move teares, yet no arte can long hold theim. For as Cicero doth saie, nothyng drieth soner, then teares, especially when we lament another mans cause, and be sory with him for his sake' (Wilson 1553 p 274).

Given these remarks, there can be little doubt about what later writers, such as Thomas Wright, meant when they advocated that prospective orators should observe people 'appassionate,' taking note of 'how they demeane themselves in passions, and observe what and how they speake in mirth, sadnesse, ire, feare, hope, &c, what motions are stirring in the eyes, hands, bodie, &c' (1604 p 179). Orators, it would seem, should imitate real life, but in doing this Wright also recommends that they temper excessive behaviour with prudence (1604 p 179). Wright's attitude finds precedence in Quintilian, who said that true emotion, such as grief, anger, and indignation, lacks art and needs to be formed by methodical training (xi pp 276–7). Wright's contention is confirmed by his contemporary William Shakespeare and much later by Michel Le Faucheur.

Shakespeare describes moderation in acting in *The Tragedie of Hamlet*: 'For in the verie Torrent, Tempest, and (as I may say) the Whirle-winde of Passion, you must acquire and beget a Temperance that may give it Smoothnesse ... Sute the Action to the Word, the Word to the Action, with this speciall observance: That you ore-step not the modestie of Nature; for any thing so over-done, is from the purpose of Playing, whose end both at the first and now, was and is, to hold as 'twer the Mirrour up to Nature; to shew Vertue her owne Feature, Scorne her owne Image, and the verie Age and Bodie of the Time, his forme and pressure' (1623 III ii, p 266). And Le Faucheur maintained that one should use *'plausible Pronunciation* and *Gesture'* because *'pronunciation* ought to be *natural*, and we must do as *Nature* dictates: For the nearer it comes up to *Nature*, the more *perfect* it is; and the further off from it, the more *vicious'* (1657 pp 31, 76). In other words, orators, and singers for that matter, should imagine themselves to be in the situation of the person they are representing, uttering the very same words that that person would have said. Their external actions should be modelled on people 'appassionate' so that voice and gesture unite to portray the thoughts and emotions of their texts convincingly. John Brinsley encapsulates the approach as follows: 'Cause them to utter every dialogue lively, as if they themselves were the persons which did speake in that dialogue, & so in every other speech, to imagine themselves to have occasion to utter the very same things' (1612 p 212). But as no one could imitate real life truly effectively by reading aloud from a book, orators spoke from memory, freeing themselves from the written page in order to concentrate on matching their style of delivery to the affections contained in their texts.[4]

Between voice and gesture, the two subdivisions of *pronunciatio*, the voice was considered the more important intermediary between speaker and listener, for as Quintilian states even gesture was adapted to it (XI pp 250–1, 276–9). Because of this pre-eminence, treatises on rhetoric often devoted a great deal of space to the voice. And in keeping with traditional rhetorical teaching, the first aspect of the voice that deserves our attention concerns the techniques by which orators and singers articulated the structure of their discourses so that listeners could easily comprehend the thoughts and emotions of the texts.[5]

✠ *To Sing Eloquently*

'All the Senses Satisfied'

Distinctions or points in sentences (punctuation to us)[6] were the vehicles through which orators articulated the structure of their sentences and paragraphs, and the observance of punctuation was considered vital to an effective delivery. Writers throughout the hundred-year period surrounding 1600, that is, from John Hart in 1551 to John Smith in 1657, regularly referred to the important role distinctions played in speaking. Francis Clement (1587 pp 24–5) maintained that by pointing sentences 'the breath is relieved, the meaning conceived, the eye directed, the eare delited, and all the senses satisfied.' And John Smith (1657 postscript) considered ignorance of points to be not only an obstacle to discerning the elegance of writing but also a hindrance to perceiving the scope, drift, and sense of an author. Still other writers, such as Thomas Heywood (1612 f c3v), considered the art of speaking well and with judgment to consist of, among other things, heeding commas, colons, full points, parentheses, breathing spaces, and distinctions. Proper pronunciation of distinctions, then, organized and paced the delivery of ideas and emotions and allowed the orator to speak elegantly, helping him create the eloquent discourse he needed to move the affections of his listeners. His style of articulation was modelled on people 'appassionate,' that is, modelled on the speech of someone in the appropriate state of mind. Imitation of real life, as noted earlier, was strongly advocated in the early seventeenth century,[7] and the observance of punctuation had become a prime component of what John Greene (1615 p 18) referred to as 'good delivery of words.' Pointing was, in short, one of the many techniques upon which the orator drew when feigning the affections of the character he was representing.

The term distinction encompassed a number of different symbols and usually consisted of the following elements:[8]

1) *comma/subdistinctio/*subdistinction or the rest [,]
2) *colon/media distinctio/*middle distinction or the joint [:]
3) *periodus/plena ac perfecta distinctio* or *comprehentio/*full
   and perfect distinction or the point [.]
4) *interrogatio/*interrogation or the asker [?]
5) *admiratio/*admiration or exclamation or the wonderer [!]
6) *parenthesis/interpositio/* interlocution or the closer [()]

To this list, some writers (notably Granger 1616, Butler 1633, and Smith 1657) add a relative of the colon – the *semicolon/semi-media distinctio/* imperfect colon [;]. The comma, the shortest rest in reading, was near the time of a crotchet (Hart 1551 p 157) and was pronounced with a little pause, with or without a breath. It signified that the sentence was unfinished, momentarily suspending the sense in such a way that that which follows ought presently to succeed. The colon was a longer rest than the comma, Hart stating that it was double the value, comparable to a minim (1551 p 160). It gave the expectation that much more was to be spoken and divided the sentence into equal or nearly equal principal parts. In delivering the last word just before the colon, Charles Butler suggests that unlike the comma, where no change in tone of voice (that is, pitch inflection and volume[9]) was required, the colon called for the speaker to let the tone of voice fall below its ordinary tenor (1633 pp 58, 59). The semicolon, on the other hand, was considered an imperfect colon and represented a pause somewhat longer than a comma but shorter than the colon itself, and like the comma no change in tone of voice was required (Butler 1633 p 59). The period was used when the sentence was fully or perfectly finished and such a pause enabled the listener to reflect upon the entire sentence in order to gain a full comprehension of it. Moreover, John Smith (1657 postscript) cautions that this pause should not be any shorter than the ear expects, and Butler advises that the tone of voice should fall on the last word and be followed by a long pause (1633 p 58).

Interrogation and exclamation are additions to the period, interrogation denoting a question and exclamation being used when a sentence, to borrow the words of John Hart, 'cometh by a sodein and great moving, of the vital and lively powers: by wondring or fearing, by myrth, sorow or anger, which are interjections: as O! phi! alas! and ho!' (1551 p 160). To this list of affections suitable for exclamatory delivery, may be added the following: admiration, indignation, exoptation, desperation, exultation, lamentation, terror, and commiseration (Butler 1633 p 61). Hart maintains that both interrogations and exclamations begin sharply (loudly) and end in a lower tune (pitch and volume), according to the length of the sentence. And even when these types of sentences contain only one word, they still should be delivered sharply (1551 p 160). In contrast, sentences ending with a normal full point must not have had their opening words uttered sharply, for Hart contends 'their tunes [that is, the pitch and volume of interrogations and exclamations] doe differ from our other maner of pronunciation at the beginning of the sentence' (1569 p 200). Butler concurs: 'Ecphonesis [exclamation] falleth as a period, and raiseth the tone in the particle of Exclamation, [o, oh, ah, alas, fi upon, out upon:] or, for want of such, in soom Emphatical woord: and always requireth a louder sound; and, when it maketh perfect sens, pauseth as a Period: ... Erotesis [interrogation], ... if it begin with a woord interrogative; as, [who, what, how, where, when, why, &c;] it falleth as a Period, and raiseth the tone in the Interrogative: as *Luk* 17, 17. Were there not ten clensed: but where are the nine?' (1633 p 61). He also maintains that when interrogation is 'urging' or is 'earnest Avouching the contrari,' such as in the phrases 'Ar yee so without understanding also?' [urging] and 'Can the blinde lead the blinde: shall they not bothe fall into the ditch?' [earnest Avouching the contrari], the sound of the voice is strained throughout the whole interrogation (1633 pp 60–1). Parenthesis, on the other hand, enabled writers to insert some other matter into a sentence, almost as an aside, which is so short that its omission would not harm the sense of the rest of the sentence. Through his tone of pronunciation, the speaker would differentiate the bracketed words from the other parts of the sentence, Richard Mulcaster (1582 p 167) suggesting that one deliver them with a lower (pitch and volume) and quicker voice. Butler corroborates Mulcaster's observation, commenting that 'parenthesis is wholely sounded with a lower voice' (1633 p 62).

Undoubtedly, a good knowledge of punctuation was common among educated classes in English society (pointing being fundamentally important to speaking and writing well), and Charles Butler and Thomas Morley disclosed the parallels between grammatical and musical punctuation. In a discussion of distinctions for both ditti (words) and harmony, Butler equated rests and cadences in music to the punctuation used in writing and oratory (1636 p 97). For just as the ditti is distinguished with points (period, colon, semicolon, and comma), he begins, so is the harmony distinguished with pauses and cadences. Semibreve rests, one or more, correspond to a period or colon, whereas minim and crotchet rests equate to semicolons, commas, breathings, and sighs. This notion is confirmed by Thomas Morley, who states that 'you may set a crotchet or minime rest above a coma or colon, but a longer rest then that of a minime you may not make till the sentence bee perfect, and then at a full point you may set what number of rests you will. Also when you would expresse sighes, you may use the crotchet or minime rest at the most, but a longer then a minime rest you may not use, because it will rather seeme a breth taking then a sigh' (1597 p 178). In other words, Butler and Morley recommend not only paralleling points in the sentences of the text with appropriate rests in the music but also expressing sighs with rests. When pronouncing a sigh, an audible breath needs to be taken at the rest, for a sigh seems to have meant inhalation rather than exhalation. In reference to sighing, William Shakespeare wrote in *The First Part of King Henry the Fourth* 'a plague of sighing and griefe, it blowes a man up like a Bladder' (1623 ii iv, p 58).

Similarly, Butler continues, perfect primary cadences, which close the harmony, equal the periods of the ditti, both within it and at the end. Secondary perfect cadences, on the other hand, correspond to colons or interrogations, but improper and imperfect cadences equate to the points of imperfect sense, that is, commas and semicolons.[10] These directions, he closes, once observed (but with discretion) will help a great deal in making the sense of the ditti obvious and comprehensible. Again, Thomas Morley concurs: 'You must not make a close (especiallie a full close) till the full sence of the words be perfect: so that keeping these rules you shall have a perfect agreement, and as it were a harmonicall concent [state of accordance] betwixt the matter and the musicke, and likewise you shall bee perfectly understoode of the auditor what you sing, which is one of the highest degrees of praise which a musicion in dittying can attaine unto or wish for' (1597 p 178).

Butler and Morley are, of course, not breaking new ground here, for their understanding of grammatical and musical punctuation is traditional, paralleling that given many years earlier by the Italian theorist Gioseffo Zarlino (1558 III chaps 53–4). In fact, Butler's subdivision of cadences into perfect, imperfect, primary, and secondary categories will be assimilated more readily if these terms are placed in their late sixteenth-century context. Zarlino, like Butler and Morley, drew upon his knowledge of grammatical punctuation to formulate a theory of musical cadences.[11] He defined the cadence as a certain action that the voices perform together, which denotes either a general repose of the harmony or the perfection of the sense of the words upon which the piece is composed. He expanded this definition by stating that the cadence is a certain termination of one part of a larger composition at a midpoint, at a distinction of the argument of the oration, or at a final termination. The cadence, he maintained, is equivalent to the *punto* (punctuation) of an oration and could be called the *punto* of musical composition. Zarlino equated these resting points to the way one pauses in the argument of an oration, not only at a middle distinction but also at a final distinction.

In conclusion, Zarlino stated that cadences were invented for designating the perfection of the parts of a larger composition and for marking the ends of perfect sentences in the text. In these places, one should use an absolute *(assolutamente)* or perfect *(perfetta)* cadence on an octave or unison (see Ex 2.1). But for middle distinctions of harmony and text, that is, when sentences have not reached final perfection, one should use an imperfect *(imperfette)* or improper *(impropiamente)* cadence on a third, fifth, sixth, or other similar consonance. This is called avoiding the cadence *(fuggir la Cadenza)*, and in these avoided cadences, the voices appear to be proceeding to a perfect cadence but turn elsewhere instead (see Ex 2.2).

Ex 2.1 Perfect cadences, Zarlino

Ex 2.2 Avoided cadences, Zarlino

As Butler, Morley, and Zarlino clearly demonstrate, cadences were the punctuation of music, and through them the performer made the structure of musical sentences evident to the listener. When these distinctions were observed, the meaning could be conceived and the senses could be satisfied. It follows, then, even though Butler, Morley, and Zarlino did not state so directly, that punctuation in the ditti implied inserting pauses of varying lengths in musical sentences: a short pause (perhaps the value of a crotchet) for a comma, a somewhat longer pause (possibly a minim) for a colon, and an even longer pause (maybe a semibreve) for a period.

Several principles emerge from the theory surrounding grammatical and musical punctuation that pertain to a reconstruction of the practices associated with eloquent singing. First, and most important, singers must observe the punctuation of the text, articulating their musical discourses in the same way that orators pointed sentences. Of course, in the real world of musical composition, as opposed to the theoretical models propounded by Butler, Morley, and Zarlino, musical cadences and rests do not always coincide with punctuation in the text, especially in the subsequent verses of strophic song. Nonetheless, wherever possible one should insert pauses of varying lengths into the musical fabric to correspond to the points in the text. In Dowland's solo songs, for example, either he already had added punctuation to the voice part by incorporating rests at the time of composition, or he provided enough leeway in the song for the singer to be able to insert pauses during performance. This last observation includes certain types of punctuation no longer commonly used in England, notably the comma just before the penultimate word of a series, that is, just before the 'and' or the 'or.' The pronunciation of this final comma contributes greatly to the vehement effect of figures such as *auxesis*, because it detaches and draws attention to the most important word of the figure. But this comma is present, and therefore probably should be pronounced, in other sorts of sentences which list things as well. For example, Dowland uses it in 'Times eldest sonne' (1600 no 6) to separate each element in the lines 'olde age the heyre of ease, Strengths foe, loves woe, and foster to devotion,' 'But thinks sighes, teares, vowes, praiers, and sacrifices,' and 'As good as showes, maskes, justes, or tilt devises.'

Second, this approach usually requires us to abandon twentieth-century editions in favour of original manuscripts or prints, for present-day editors sometimes 'modernize' and 'regularize' punctuation. This unfortunate practice distorts one of the most potent tools singers possess for impressing the meaning of their sentences upon listeners. Notable exceptions to this practice are David Scott's edition of Thomas Campion's *First Book of Ayres* and *Second Book of Ayres* (1979a, 1979b) and Philip Brett's recent edition of some of William Byrd's sacred music (1989). Scott retains the original punctuation, stating 'in the songs this [the original punctuation] may be an indication of phrasing, and must not be ignored' (p vii). Brett considers the punctuation carefully and at times follows his source literally, especially when the composer has adopted an unusual punctuation (p xxiv).[12]

Third, the style of delivery used by English singers from the late sixteenth and early seventeenth centuries obviously was highly articulated. Seamless delivery within musical sentences and paragraphs seems foreign to the era. Fourth, pointing sentences helps eliminate one of the main problems in performing strophic song – moving the affections of the listeners in second or third verses when each new strophe is sung to the same short, simple tune. Because the punctuation in most songs differs for each verse and follows the dramatic unfolding of the poem's story, singers can create interest simply by adhering to the points that are marked in the sources,[13] and nowhere is this more evident than in the strophic songs from Dowland's *The First Booke of Songes*, especially in 'Awake, sweet love' and 'His golden locks.'

The First Booke of Songes initially was published in 1597 and enjoyed four reprints over the next 16 years (1600, 1603, 1606, and 1613).[14] The 1606 issue contained important revisions, repeated in the 1613 printing, in which someone significantly altered the punctuation in the songs. We do not know who made these revisions, but Diana Poulton persuasively argues that it was Dowland himself (1982 p 217). If her hypothesis is correct (and I believe that it probably is) Dowland sought to improve the punctuation in certain songs, strengthening the hierarchical relationship between the points. By doing this, he allowed the structure of the sentences to be easily discerned and provided a more detailed guide for singers to follow. New commas were added, and many of the commas in the earlier editions were converted to the longer pauses of the colon or period. These changes provide better satisfaction for the ear, to borrow Francis Clement's words (1587 pp 24–5), and clearly distinguish the parts of the sentences from one another, making the meaning readily apparent. Without this 'tunable uttering of our words and sentences' (Mulcaster 1582 p 166), which brings 'the matter, much the readier to the senses' (Hart 1569 p 199), one would find it almost impossible to move the affections of others, for a good command of punctuation is one of the main components in the art of speaking, and by extrapolation, singing well.

In 'Awake, sweet love,' for example, the emended punctuation orders the parts of the sentences into their proper relationship and indicates the emphasis the singer should give the various members. Commas are used to separate what John Hart refers to as 'short saings' in which 'the matter hangeth loking for more to be said' (1551 p 159), and semicolons, colons, and periods further articulate the unfolding of the sense of the sentences. A comparison of the 1597 and 1613 versions of the first verse will demonstrate how the later punctuation aids delivery (see Ex 2.3).

Ex 2.3 'Awake, sweet love,' first verse

1597	1613
Awake sweet love thou art returnd,	Awake, sweet love, thou art returnd:
My hart which long in absence mournd	My hart, which long in absence mournd,
Lives nowe in perfect joy,	Lives now in perfect joy.
Let love which never absent dies,	Let love, which never absent dies,
Now live for ever in her eyes	Now live for ever in her eyes,
When came my first anoy,	Whence came my first annoy.
Only herselfe hath seemed faire,	Only herselfe hath seemed faire:
She only I could love,	She only I could love,
She onely drave me to dispaire	She only drave me to despaire,
When she unkind did prove.	When she unkind did prove.
Dispayer did make me wish to die	Despaire did make me wish to die;
That I my joyes might end,	That I my joyes might end:
She onely which did make me flie	She only, which did make me flie,
My state may now amend.	My state may now amend.

If we observe the punctuation in the ways described by Hart, Mulcaster, Smith, and others and use the tone of voice (volume) they suggest for differentiating the various members of a sentence, we are able to begin to recreate the style of delivery that probably was common in Dowland's lifetime. The first two periods of 'Awake, sweet love' might be read/sung as follows (larger type represents the main sense of the sen-

Ex 2.4 'Awake, sweet love,' periods one and two

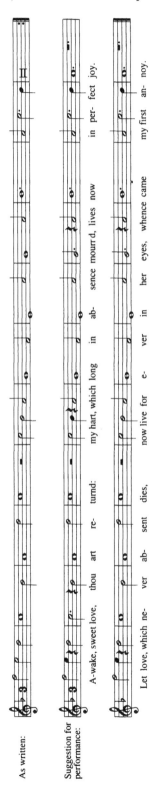

tence and smaller type indicates what Dowland must have considered to be 'short saings,' uttered with a lower [quieter] voice, which interrupt yet expand the overall meaning):

> Awake, sweet love, thou art returnd:
> My hart, which long in absence mournd,
>   Lives now in perfect joy.
> Let love, which never absent dies,
> Now live for ever in her eyes,
>   Whence came my first annoy.

In uttering these sentences, singers not only would distinguish the parts by means of dynamic shading but also would incorporate the textual articulations into the musical line. In Example 2.4, I have followed the advice of Hart and Butler and equated commas with crotchet rests (in one case, I have retained Dowland's minim rest), colons with minim rests, and periods with semibreve rests.[15] This approach enables performers to enliven their delivery even when, as the example demonstrates, the poem progresses to new words and thoughts while the music repeats. Careful observance of points, then, coupled with changing the tone of voice (volume) to suit the hierarchical importance of each member within those points, coherently arranges the ideas in the poem and creates variety; this helps to project the story and the affections contained therein to the listener.

In other strophic songs, such as 'His golden locks,' the punctuation in the 1613 edition (see Ex 2.5) demonstrates that, even though the points provide a remarkably clear plan for pacing the projection of the story, Dowland conceived the vocal line in terms of the punctuation of the first verse alone. This, of course, presents obstacles for singers to overcome in delivering the second and third verses, particularly in the last two lines of each verse, and highlights the inherent difficulty performers face in making strophic songs dramatically convincing.

Ex 2.5 'His golden locks' 1613

(variants in punctuation from 1597 are in square brackets)[16]

His golden locks time hath to silver turnde. [,]
O time too swift, O swiftnesse never ceasing! [,]
His youth gainst time & age hath ever spurnd,
But spurnd in vain, youth waneth by increasing. [:]
    Beautie, strength, youth are flowers but fading seene: [,]
    Dutie, Faith, Love are roots and ever greene.

His helmet now shall make a hive for Bees,
And lovers Sonets turne to holy Psalmes:
A man at armes must now serve on his knees,
And feed on prayers which are ages almes: [,]
    But though from Court to cotage he depart, [no
        punctuation]
    His Saint is sure of his unspotted heart.

And when he saddest sits in homely Cell,
Hee'l teach his swaines this Caroll for a song,
Blest be the hearts that wish my Soveraigne well,
Curst be the soule that thinks her any wrong. [:]
    Goddes allow this aged man his right,
    To be your Beadsman now that was your Knight.

The poem recounts the plight of an aging knight, who after a life of dedicated service seeks a position more suited to his advanced years. As in 'Awake, sweet love,' Dowland has strengthened the punctuation, substituting periods for commas and colons and appropriately turning the second line of the first verse into an exclamation. Yet only in the first verse do the points suit the vocal line perfectly, and this confirms my contention that Dowland conceived the music in terms of the first verse alone (see Ex 2.6). The music Dowland composed for the exclamation 'O time too swift, O swiftnesse never ceasing!' is the melodic equivalent of John Hart's sharp beginning followed by a lower ending. The comma is accommodated easily in the vocal line, as it helps the singer (and listener) prepare for the repetition of the exclamtory 'O!'. However, this musical period works imperfectly for the second and third verses, the corresponding lines of these verses being single, longer units of thought without emotional outburst:

> *Verse 2*:   And lovers Sonets turne to holy Psalmes:
> *Verse 3*:   Hee'l teach his swaines this Carroll for a song.

A similar problem occurs with the melody Dowland composed for the fourth line of the first verse. The two members from verse one, 'but spurnd in vain, youth waneth by increasing,' fit the music well (see Ex 2.6), the antithetical nature of the melody, the first part rising and the second falling, paralleling the sense of these members (that is, their cause and effect relationship) and the comma providing the natural break both text and music require. But once again, the second and third verses are ill served by a melody designed as a bipartite structure:

> *Verse 2*:   And feed on prayers which are ages almes:
> *Verse 3*:   Curst be the soule that thinks her any wrong.

Ex 2.6 'His golden locks,' first verse

Ex 2.7 'His golden locks,' final periods of verses two and three

Verse 2:	But	though from	Court to	cot- age	he de-	part,	His	Saint	is	sure of his un- spot- ted heart.
Verse 3:	God-	des al-	low this	a- ged	man his	right,	To	be	your Beads-man now that was your Knight.

Yet the greatest problem for the singer in subsequent verses lies in the music written for the last two lines of the first verse – music which is so perfectly suited to the text that one can hardly imagine other words being adapted to it. The contrast between the two members of this period, the first one detailing what once was and the second listing those unwavering qualities which are ever present, is reflected in Dowland's melodic setting (see Ex 2.6). The first part begins with a repetition of the final of the mode and comes to rest on the transitory cadence note A which, like the colon it represents, gives the expectation that much more is to be spoken. The second part fulfils this anticipation, as it begins a fifth above the final and maintains a somewhat higher tessitura, gradually bringing the musical thought to a full and perfect close with a cadence on G, the structural foundation of the mode. Singers achieve their most persuasive delivery of this period when the words, through the observation of the rhetorical figure *articulus*, are separated from one another by pronouncing the commas. This approach draws attention to and emphasizes each quality in the list. Undoubtedly, Dowland designed his melody with this form of delivery in mind, for he employs the longer note values of semibreve and minim to set the words in the list, notes which by their very nature, especially when delivered slowly, are emphasized and separated by commas.[17] The corresponding lines of the poem in the second and third verses, however, are constructed totally differently:

> *Verse 2:*   But though from Court to cotage he depart,
> His Saint is sure of his unspotted heart.
> *Verse 3:*   Goddes allow this aged man his right,
> To be your Beadsman now that was
> your Knight.

They are, to borrow musical terminology, through composed and lack the accumulation of like words *(synathroismos)* which characterizes the first verse. Each member drives forward, requiring only one articulation at the midpoint. The melody is, unfortunately, most inappropriate for these sentences; the semibreves and minims which suited the first verse so well halt the forward motion in the second and third verses, producing an unnatural declamation of the text (see Ex 2.7).

Dowland's brilliance as a song-writer is shown in his highly imaginative and thoroughly convincing setting of the first verse, and the problems I have identified in subsequent verses are by no means insurmountable. The second lines of verses two and three require singers to perceive the melody as one long unit rather than as two separate members of a period. The fourth lines of verses two and three are even less problematical to deliver because the dividing point in Dowland's melody occurs in each case just before a relative pronoun (which or that) – places which can withstand the slight articulation implied in the melody. But the final periods of verses two and three are not remedied so easily, for it is impossible to completely reverse the halting effect of the semibreves. Singers may wish, however, to give at least some sense of forward motion to the line through a slight dynamic swelling on the first semibreve of each member.

Persuasive delivery in the late sixteenth and early seventeenth centuries presupposed a knowledge of punctuation, and singers needed to be thoroughly familiar with the purpose and pronunciation of distinctions. Dowland's emendations to punctuation in the later printings of *The First Booke of Songes*, besides ensuring that the published editions reflected his conception of the songs more precisely, demonstrate how points could control compositional style by suggesting melodic figures which would enhance, at least in first verses, the projection of the affections contained in the poem. Punctuation made musical discourse intelligible and through its observance the meaning could be conceived, the ear delighted, and all the senses satisfied. Without correct utterance of punctuation, to paraphrase Quintilian, all the other merits of oratory are worth nothing (xi pp 262–3).

Pronouncing Distinctly

Clarity of delivery depended on two things: punctuation, as we have just seen, and another equally important factor, enunciation (Quintilian XI pp 260–1). From at least Quintilian's time, rhetoricians stressed the necessity of uttering words distinctly, later English writers repeating anecdotes about the methods of correcting poor enunciation that were centuries old. In 1553, Thomas Wilson told the story of Demosthenes who, being unable to pronounce the letter 'r,' practised speaking with little stones under his tongue until he spoke as plainly as any other man (p 433). Musicians in England, Wilson continues, used to resort to a similar custom; that is, they placed gags in the mouths of children 'that they might pronounce distinctely.' But, alas, he bemoans the loss of this tradition in his own time (p 433).

Improper enunciation was a common fault in speaking, and Wilson provides us with two examples of typical problems. He tells of a priest, as nice as a 'Nonnes Henne,' who had such bad diction that he would say *Dominus vobicum* for *Dominus vobiscum*, while others say 'blacke vellet' instead of 'blacke velvet' (p 434). The confusion this indistinct speech would cause in listeners is obvious, and it is the dangers of poor enunciation which probably led Charles Butler to advise singers 'to sing as plainly as they woolde speak: pronouncing every Syllable and letter (specially the Vouels) distinctly and treatably ... [so that] ... the Ditti (which is half the grace of the Song) may bee known and understood' (1636 p 98). The foundation of persuasive discourse, then, in both speaking and singing consisted of clarity in delivery, that is, words uttered distinctly and sentences articulated carefully in order that the sense of the text could be assimilated easily by listeners. John Brinsley recommends that schoolchildren learn to utter every syllable 'truly, plainly, fully, and distinctly' so that 'others who heare may understand' (1612 p 17), and in analysing sentences (Brinsley's term), students should observe all the points in order to 'see and consider both the beginning, middest, and end of the sentence together; and also each clause in it' (1612 p 95). Once these basic principles of eloquent delivery had been mastered, the orator/singer was in a position to explore the many techniques for enlivening discourse.

'Figures and Passionate Ornaments Made Manifest'

The voice possesses an infinite variety of expression (Quintilian xi pp 252–3), and orators and singers adjusted the nature and quality of the voice to suit the affections they were to portray (Wright 1604 p 180). Poetry, discourses, orations, etc were constructed from many smaller parts, each with its own affection, and every part required individual treatment in delivery (p 180). Even when the overall effect of a text could be assigned to a single passion, orators often used elements of contrast within the text to help them persuade listeners (p 180). And in order to capture the minds of listeners with texts 'woven with various periods, and compounded of sundry parts' (p 180), orators made their utterance conform to the structure of the text, following principles of delivery which dated back to ancient times. In discussing the attributes of good reading, Quintilian listed the three main components of speaking that enabled orators to create the variety so necessary for persuasive utterance. One should avoid monotony, he suggested, by raising or lowering the voice (modulating it within each phrase), by increasing or slackening speed, and by speaking with greater or lesser energy (i pp 146–7 and xi pp 266–7). Without this approach to delivering the various members within sentences (even when a member consisted of just one word), every word in the discourse would appear to be of equal importance (xi pp 268–71). To these three tenets of good speaking, later English writers added the notion of altering the tonal quality of the voice, as the time and cause required, to produce a delivery which was 'now harshe and hard, now smoothe and sweete' (Mulcaster 1581 p 58). Quintilian's three components of speaking were discussed in the middle of the seventeenth century by Michel Le Faucheur, who stated that the voice had three principal 'differences' – highness or lowness, vehemence or softness, and swiftness or slowness (1657 p 80). In order to avoid monotony, these elements were to be varied 'according to the quality of the *Subjects* he [the orator] treats of, the nature of the *Passions* he would shew in *himself* or raise in *others*, the several parts of his *Discourse*, the different *Figures* he makes use of, and the *variety* of his *words* and his *Phrase*' (1657 pp 92–3).

Of these principles, the only ones which singers did not control were modulation of pitch and the metrical rate at which words were delivered, because in songs these two elements were pre-determined by the composer's melody. They did, however, exercise complete control over many important aspects of delivery and could vary speed (tempo), volume (dynamics), and tonal quality of the voice to accommodate the affections present in each section of the song. This type of approach was as necessary in singing as it was in speaking, for songs performed in a single tempo with a restricted dynamic range and no change in tonal quality of the voice would have been considered monotonous and clearly would have been incapable of inflaming the passions of listeners. John Dowland captured the essence of the singer's task with the advice 'Let every Singer conforme his voyce to the words, that as much as he can make the *Concent* [the state of accordance between words and voice] sad when the words are sad; & merry, when they are merry' (Dowland 1609 p 89). This style of singing seems to have been practised in Italy as well, for in 1588 Gioseffo Zarlino recommended that singers vary the tonal quality of their voices in the same way that orators did:

> Con alta voce & horribile, gridando & esclamando, esprimere il suo concetto; & questo quando parla di cose, con lequali egli voglia indur spavento & terrore; & tallor con voce sommessa & bassa; quando vuole indur commiseratione, cosi non è cosa disconvenevole al Musico, d'usar simili attioni, nell'acuto & nel grave, hora con voce alta, & hora con voce sommessa, recitando le sue Compositioni … onde non dico, che'l Cantore cantando debba ne gridare, ne far strepito: percioche non è cosa habbia ne proportione, ne decoro … cosi se questo si permette al Recitante per il commodo de gli Ascol tanti; si permetterà anco al Cantore alcune attioni nel Cantare / [Sometimes the orator speaks] with a loud and horrible voice, shouting and exclaiming, to express his thoughts. And this he does when he speaks of things with which he wishes to induce fear and terror, and

at other times he uses a soft and low voice when he wishes to induce commiseration. Thus, it is not an unbecoming thing for a musician to use similar procedures [attioni – changes in volume and tonal quality of the voice] in the high and low [pitches], [to sing] now with a loud voice, now with a subdued voice, as he recites his compositions ... Thus, I do not say that the singer should either shout or roar in singing, because these things have neither proportion nor decorum ... Just as the reciter is permitted to do this [change his volume and the tonal quality of his voice] for the benefit of the listeners, so the singer also is permitted some [of these] procedures in singing. (1588 p 319)

The passions in a piece of music changed rapidly, just as in oration, for as Richard Hooker states, 'whether it [the passion embodied in the 'artificiall musick' to which psalms are set] resemble unto us the same state wherein our mindes alreadie are, or a cleane contrarie, we are not more contentedly by the one confirmed, then changed and led away by the other' (1597 p 75). Obviously, this required singers to alter their style of delivery quickly from one phrase to another, ensuring that, lest the mind of the speaker appear 'unnaturall and distracted,' they portrayed one passion at a time. Only when the *'Words, Tone, Greatnesse* of the Voice [and] *Gesture* of the body and Countenance' proceeded from a single passion was the text considered to be well pronounced (Hobbes 1637 p 108).[18] Nonetheless, a degree of gracefulness was expected in projecting rapid changes of affection, at least according to Michel Le Faucheur, for one should not vary the voice 'so very grosly *all on the sudden* like a *Thunder-Clap'* because it would surprise and displease the auditors (1657 pp 90–1). Le Faucheur's statement, however, must be qualified by other passages in his book where he advocates that orators imitate real life in the same way that actors do and come as close as possible to natural pronunciation by changing the voice 'according to the different *quality* of *persons* and the *diversity* of *Subjects'* (pp 76–7).

Thus, a knowledge of how to match the voice to the passion that was to be represented was considered essential to eloquent delivery, and writers such as Abraham Fraunce (1588), Thomas Wright (1604), and Michel Le Faucheur (1657) specified what tonal quality of the voice was appropriate for particular passions. The list of passions these writers discuss covers a wide range of emotions and includes pity, lamentation, anger, fear, anguish, hatred, sadness, grief, joy, gladness, love, confidence, and compassion. Moreover, Thomas Wright warns that not only must the tonal quality of the voice suit the passion to be expressed but also the words spoken must be appropriate to a person in such a state of mind. His advice reminds us that an understanding of the text on all levels, that is, from surface emotional content to deeper structural elements involving rhetorical devices through which the passions are communicated to listeners, is essential to effective persuasion. Wright gives a humorous anecdote to underscore the importance of matching words and style of delivery to the passion embodied in the subject. One would not, he asserts, advise a neighbour of a fire in his house by saying to him: 'O deare neighbour, although I am far unfit by eloquence, to perswade you to looke to your house, and carefully to watch about it, lest fire fall upon it, as now of late I perceive it hath done, therfore provide water & succour, for otherwise both all your goods and mine will bee consumed' (1604 pp 181–2). The absurdity of this speech is obvious. It is unnatural and does not portray fear and danger realistically; rather, the speech and style of delivery should represent someone in that state of mind more accurately: 'He would runne crying into the street, fire, fire, help, help, water, water, succour, succour, alas, alas, we are undone, quickly, speedily, run for ladders, pull downe this rafter, cut that beame, untile the house; what meane you, stirre hands, armes, and legs, hie thee for water, run thou for yron crookes, and hookes: hast, hast, wee are all undone' (p 182). Words such as these when uttered with an appropriate pacing, tonal quality of the voice, and so on would succeed in moving the passions of others, inciting them to action.

In general, the tonal quality of the voice to be employed in any given passage was based on an observation of people 'appassionate,' Michel Le Faucheur emphasizing that the orator must 'first consider the thing he's to speak of, with care, and carry a deep impression of it in his *mind*, before he be either sensibly touch'd with it *himself* or able to move *others* upon it with a more effectual *Sympathy*' (1657 p 97). Le Faucheur summarizes his guiding principle as follows: 'If your *Speech* proceeds from a *violent Passion*, it produces a *violent Pronunciation;* if it comes from a *Peaceable* and *Gentle Thought*, the *Pronunciation* again is as *Peaceable, Gentle* and *Calm:* So that the *Orator* would do well to adjust every *Tone* and *Accent* of his *Voyce* to each *Passion* that afflicts or overjoys him, which he would raise in *others* to a degree of *Sympathy*' (1657 p 99). The various recommendations of Fraunce, Wright, and Le Faucheur are contained in Table 2.1.

In addition to describing the tonal quality of the voice that suits individual passions, one of these writers, Abraham Fraunce, provides specific examples from Sir Philip Sydney (and other authors) of the kinds of texts that carry particular pronunciations. A full, sobbing, flexible, and interrupted voice (suitable for pity and lamentation) would be employed in the sentence 'Ah silly soule, that couldest please thy selfe with so impossible imagination' (1588 f 13r). But in anger, a shrill, sharp, quick, and short voice works well for the words spoken by a man who was thought to have been incapable of controlling his wife: 'What, shall my Wife bee my Mistresse? Thinke you not that thus much time hath taught mee to rule her? I will mewe the Gentlewoman till shee have cast all her feathers, if shee rowse her selfe against mee' (f 14r). Fear and bashfulness produced a contracted, stammering, and trembling voice, as in 'Alas how painfull a thing it is to a divided minde to make a well joyned aunswere?' (f 14v). However, the opposite, that is a tender, mild, and sweetly flowing voice, suited passages dealing with joy, gladness, or pleasure:

> Lock up faire lidds, the treasures of my heart,
> Preserve those beames, this ages onlie light:
> To her sweet sence, sweet sleepe, some ease impart,
> Her sence too weake to beare her spirits might. &c. (f J1r)

Similarly, a smoothing and submissive voice served passions concerned with desiring, soothing, flattering, yielding, and gratifying: 'By the happie woman that bare thee, by all the joyes of thy heart, and successe of thy desire, I beseech thee, turne thy selfe into some consideration of me, and

Table 2.1 Passions and tonal quality of the voice

Passion	Fraunce (1588)	Wright (1604)	Le Faucheur (1657)
pity and lamentation	full, sobbing, flexible, interrupted	—	—
anger	shrill, sharp, quick, short	—	sharp, impetuous, violent, taking breath often and speaking short upon the passion
fear	contracted, stammering, trembling	small, trembling	trembling, stammering
bashfulness	contracted, stammering, trembling	—	—
anguish	'a hollow voyce fetcht from the bottome of the throate, groaning'	—	—
hatred	—	loud, sharp	sharp, sullen, severe
ire	—	loud, sharp	—
sadness and commiseration	—	grave, doleful, plain, interrupted with woeful exclamations	—
grief	'a hollow voyce fetcht from the bottome of the throate, groaning'	—	dull, languishing and sad moan, sometimes breaking off abruptly with a sob and fetching up a sigh or groan from the heart
compassion	—	—	very soft, submissive, pitiful
joy	tender, mild, sweetly flowing	plain, pleasant, soft, mild, gentle	full, flowing, brisk
gladness and pleasure	tender, mild, sweetly flowing	—	—
desiring	smoothing and submissive	plain, pleasant, soft, mild, gentle	—
soothing, flattering, yielding, gratifying	smoothing and submissive	—	—
love	—	plain, pleasant, soft, mild, gentle	soft, gay, charming
confidence	—	—	loud and strong

rather shewe pitie, in now helping me, than in too late repenting my death, which hourlie threatens me' (f J2v). But for some of the more pitiful utterances born from anguish and grief, 'a hollow voyce fetcht from the bottome of the throate, groaning' was appropriate, as in 'O Deserts, Deserts, how fit a guest am I for you? since my heart is fuller of wild ravenous beasts, than ever you were' (f J1). These descriptions of the voice have a direct bearing on song performance, for lute-songs certainly contain exclamatory outbursts (see Exs 1.5, 1.18, 3.1, 3.2) and some of the melodies are designed so that singers may insert sighs, sobs, and groans (see Exs 1.11, 3.1, 3.2). In fact, Thomas Morley recommends representing sighs with rests of either a crotchet or a minim in duration (1597 p 178).

But beyond the specific suggestions given by Fraunce, advice of a more general nature is offered by Michel Le Faucheur (1657). In speaking of natural things, especially when it is one's intention only to make the listeners understand and no more, there is no need of any 'great *heat* or *motion* upon the matter;' a clean and distinct voice will suffice (p 93). But in speaking of the actions of men, the tonal quality of the voice must match the deed. The just and the honest should be expressed through a noble accent and through a tone of satisfaction, honour, and esteem, whereas the unjust and infamous should be expressed through a strong, violent, and passionate voice as well as through a tone of anger, disgrace, and detestation (p 94). Moreover, if one is representing a brave hero, Le Faucheur suggests using a lofty and magnificent tone (p 107), but to show contempt for a man he recommends a scornful tone without any passion, eagerness, or violence in the voice (p 110). And when one needs to complain of a barbarous injustice, an elevated tone, proportioning the vehemence and passion of the voice to the cruelty of the injury, is most appropriate (p 115). However, after one has spoken with this sort of violent passion, Le Faucheur suggests that it is best to cool the voice by lowering the tone and making it more humble (p 117). If one does not rest the voice in this way, it may suddenly fail, the voice being incapable of withstanding this violence for long periods of time (p 82).

Later in his treatise, Le Faucheur turns his attention from the general to the specific and comments upon the tonal quality of the voice required

for pronouncing individual words (1657 pp 166–8). He discusses six categories of words, describing their affective character and the utterance
suitable for each category. Emphatical words, that is, words which are
very strong and positive, should be uttered with emphasis and distinction,
that is, separated from the other words surrounding them. These are
words such as certainly, assuredly, infallibly, undoubtedly, necessarily,
absolutely, expressly, and manifestly. Terms of honour (admirable,
incredible, incomparable, ineffable, inestimable, glorious, glittering,
pompous, triumphant, illustrious, heroic, august, majestic, and adorable)
are used to praise or extol and should carry a magnificent tone. But words
such as cruel, heinous, wicked, detestable, abominable, execrable, and
monstrous are employed to dispraise and detest, and one should utter
them with a most passionate and loud voice. In dealing with sorrow, one
might choose terms of complaint or lamentation (unfortunate, miserable,
fatal, mournful, pitiful, deplorable, and lamentable), and these must be
pronounced with a melancholy accent. Similarly, words of weak, imperfect, or languishing resentment should have a doleful, moaning accent as
well as a low and slow voice, as in the sentence 'When I search'd into the
Faith of my Heart, I found it so weak, so imperfect, so languishing, &c'
(pp 167–8). And in using terms of extenuation and slight (pitiful,
insignificant, little, low, mean, despicable, and feeble), employ a very low,
lessening, abject voice with an accent of the greatest scorn and disdain.
But lay more stress on words of quantity (grand, high, sublime, profound,
long, large, innumerable, and eternal) and universality (all the world,
generally, everywhere, always, and never) and pronunce the latter with 'a
certain *gravity* and *height* of *Accent*' (p 167).

Other sorts of individual words, that is, those contained in rhetorical
figures, were to be emphasized as well. John Brinsley advises: 'Let them
[schoolchildren] also be taught carefully, in what word the Emphasis
lyeth; and therefore which is to be elevated in the pronuntiation. As
namely those wordes in which the chiefe Trope or Figure is' (1612 pp
213–14). What Brinsley means by emphasis and elevation should be clear
by the preceding discussion of the techniques of varying the voice to suit
specific passions and words. Emphasis means stress, and connected to this
meaning is the figure of the same name with which one can 'inforce the

sence of any thing by a word of more than ordinary efficacie' (Puttenham 1589 p 194). Elevation refers to the change of voice which causes a word or words to be highlighted, but also it simply may mean louder.[19] Brinsley's statement is reinforced by one of Abraham Fraunce's comments on the art of eloquent speaking: 'In the particular applying of the voyce to severall words, wee make tropes that bee most excellent plainly appeare. For without this change of voyce, neither anie *Ironia*, nor lively *Metaphore* can well bee discerned' (1588 II chap 1). Moreover, a later writer, John Barton, provides an example of the figure *epizeuxis* and suggests how speakers could make it 'plainly appeare': '*Thou, thou* art worthy to be praised. As in every word some syllable is pronounced more acutely; so in every clause some word is uttered with more vehemencie then the rest, as the first 2 words in this clause must be' (1634 p 35). Speech becomes even more stirring, he continues, when a number of emphases occur in the same sentence: 'Now when we put many Emphases together, the sentence is very moving. Rom. 8.38. Neither *death*, nor *life*, nor *angels*, nor *principalities*, nor *powers*, nor *things present*, nor *things to come*, nor *height*, nor *depth*, &c. all these [words in italics] must be pronounced Emphatically' (p 35).

It is only natural, of course, that the figures of rhetoric receive this sort of treatment, for they were among the most important vehicles orators and singers possessed for inflaming the passions of listeners. But unfortunately, apart from the few scattered remarks mentioned here, English writers do not discuss the precise techniques for adjusting the voice to emphasize and elevate a wide variety of figures. In English treatises, by and large we must be content with the tantalizingly short statements of Brinsley, Fraunce, and Barton. Michel Le Faucheur, on the other hand, offers a profusion of detailed advice on the techniques of delivering no less than thirteen separate figures, some of them being the figures most frequently encountered in the lute-song repertoire. As we have seen earlier, Le Faucheur's discussion of the tonal quality of the voice appropriate for specific passions (and other similar comments on the art of delivery) is virtually identical to those of English writers. Therefore, I feel that I am on reasonably safe ground in using Le Faucheur's chapter 10, '*How to* vary *the* Voyce *according to the* Figures of Rhetorick' (1657 pp 128–50), to compensate for the deficiency of English treatises. His remarks are reinforced by Barton's discussion of *epizeuxis* cited above and on two other occasions by comments found in Peacham the Elder's revised edition of *The Garden of Eloquence* (1593). For my purposes, the most important figures Le Faucheur treats are *ecphonesis (exclamatio)*, *prosopopoeia (conformatio)*, *apostrophe (aversio)*, *parrhesia (licentia)*, *climax (gradatio)*, *aposiopesis (praecisio)*, *epizeuxis (subjunctio)*, *anaphora (repetitio)*, and *epistrophe (conversio)*, but he also discusses subjection, dialogism (conference), *antithesis (contrarium)*, and *epimone* (insistance).

With regard to *ecphonesis*, Le Faucheur recommends pronouncing exclamatory outbursts with a louder voice and a more passionate accent (1657 p 128). Peacham the Elder probably would have agreed with this advice, for he states 'The principall end and use of this figure is by the vehemency of our voice and utterance to express the greatnesse of our affections and passions, and thereby to move the like affections in our hearers' (1593 p 63). Peacham also reminds us that so vehement a form of speech should not be used without some 'great cause' and not too often, lest it become odious. In uttering *prosopopoeias*, the rhetorical equivalent of the passionate ayre in music, Le Faucheur suggests varying the voice according to the '*Diversity, Character* and *Business*' of the person the orator is feigning (1657 p 131). Related to *prosopopoeia* is *apostrophe*, a turning of one's speech to some new person in order to feign their presence (Hoskins 1599 p 162), and this, Le Faucheur asserts, demands a louder voice, as upon a sudden diversion of the speech to another person, then one can return with a lower voice as if it were a secret soliloquy or a private reflection (1657 p 133). With *parrhesia*, one takes the liberty to say everything one has a mind to say and consequently the voice must be full and loud (p 140). But in *climax* or gradation, 'where the *Discourse* climbs up by several *clauses* of a Sentence to a *Period* or Full Point; 'tis manifest that the *Voyce* must be rais'd accordingly by the same degrees of *elevation* to answer every *step* of the *Figure*, till it is at the utmost *height* of it' (p 142). Similarly, *aposiopesis* requires the parts of the figure to be differentiated one from another. In this figure, the orator pronounces the words which introduce it with the '*highest Accent*' but holds his peace and conceals what might be said further in the matter by lowering his voice a 'tone or two' for the remainder of the passage. Le Faucheur provides the following example to demonstrate his point: 'For I can say of my self [the abrupt ending of these words of the *'highest Accent'* are followed by words spoken a 'tone or two' lower]. —— But I will not say any thing *piquant* or *severe* at the beginning, though every body sees he is come to accuse me of *Alacrity* and *Lightness of Heart'* (p 143).

Other figures of a like nature that also need clear differentiation between the parts are subjection, *antithesis*, and dialogism. In subjection, several questions are asked and answers are given to each one of them. The orator delivers the figure by varying his voice so that the question is given with 'one *Tone*, and the *Answer, another*; either pronouncing the *demand* higher and the *answer* lower, or on the contrary' (p 144). Although it is not clear from Le Faucheur's discussion of this figure whether he is referring to changes in volume or changes in vehemence, his remarks on the delivery of *antithesis* specifically mention alterations in volume to distinguish the contrarieties: 'He [the orator] must distinguish upon both the *contraries*, and pronounce the *first* of 'em with a different *Tone* from the *latter; this* with a *louder Accent* than *that*, to shew the opposition betwixt the *one* and the *other* and to adjust the *voyce* to the *Contrariety'* (p 145). And in dialogism or conference the orator must change his voice in turns as if two people actually were talking together (p 135).

Le Faucheur discusses several figures of repetition, clearly indicating how the reiterated words are to be uttered. In *epizeuxis*,[20] an immediate repetition of the same word, the orator must give the restated word a 'different sound' and pronounce it 'far *louder* and *stronger*' than on its first statement (p 147). However, the opposite occurs in *anaphora* and *epistrophe*;[21] that is, the repeated words (in the former, at the beginning of successive sentences and in the latter at the end) are to be uttered with the same accent and sound, 'but in a different manner from the *Pronunciation* of all the *other parts* of the *Period*, to give the *Figure* its due *Emphasis* and *Distinction* in his Discourse' (pp 147–9). Incidentally, Le Faucheur's explanation of *anaphora* parallels a description found in a sixteenth-century music treatise for the delivery of the equivalent musical figure, *fuga* (point of imitation in modern parlance): use a clearer and more distinct voice *(voce clariore & explanata magis)* than usual for delivering *fugae;* that is, the voices in a *fuga* should stand out from that which precedes and follows the *fuga* itself (Finck 1556 v f Ss3v).[22] The last of Le Faucheur's figures, *epimone,* involves driving the argument home in several different ways, and a brisk, pressing, and insulting voice must be used for this figure (1657 p 137).

Because the voice was considered the most important intermediary between the speaker/singer and the listener, it truly must have been tuned to the heart, for only by constantly matching the voice to the various passions in the text, as dictated by specific words and figures contained in that text, could one inflame the minds of listeners. The detailed statements on the subject by Fraunce, Wright, and Le Faucheur outlined here clarify precisely what Fraunce meant when he made his rather cryptic remark, 'Nothing is either better for his voyce that speaketh, or more pleasant to the eares of them that heare, than often changing' (1588 II chap 1). And if the speaker/singer were to achieve this coveted goal, that is, if one gained the ability to make passions and figures manifest through changes to the voice, then orators and singers most certainly would have had to possess an infinite variety of expression in their voices. But this sort of eloquent delivery was not achieved, of course, without assiduous practice. Le Faucheur recommends taking a sentence and repeating it over and over until one can pronounce it 'according to *Art*' (1657 p 214), and Fraunce maintains that because 'practise and exercise is all in all: learne therfore some such speach wherein are contained all, or most varieties of voyce, and oftentimes use to pronounce the same in such order and with as great heed as if thou were to utter it in some great assemblie' (1588 f J3r). In this last regard, John Brinsley specifically mentions practising the orations of Tullie, for they contain many figures (especially 'Exclamations, Prosopopeis, Apostrophees, and the like') which will acquaint speakers with a wide variety of pronunciation (1612 p 214).

There can be no doubt about the importance of this approach to delivery in the late sixteenth and early seventeenth centuries. Passionate utterance was the crowning glory in the training of actors, lawyers, preachers, and others who sought to persuade. The techniques for capturing and inflaming the minds of listeners were well known at the time, and enough documentation survives to enable us to reconstruct with some accuracy the principles behind the art of eloquent delivery. Many of these principles are directly transferable to singing, and I believe that the principles discussed this far also formed the basis for eloquent delivery in sung discourse. In general, modern singers of seventeenth-century vocal music are not accustomed to changing the tonal quality of their voices (or style of delivery for that matter) to match the character they are portraying, but I hope that the preceding section demonstrates the importance of adopting this approach.[23] However, before turning to a discussion of gesture, the other important component of *pronunciatio*, I wish to consider that purely musical aspect of eloquent singing, the art of applying divisions and graces to a melody.

Divisions and Graces

Singers in the early seventeenth century were expected to master not only correct and persuasive utterance but also, judging by the descriptions of singing which survive, the techniques of melodic ornamentation. In 1591, the 'Dittie of *Come againe* was sung, with excellent division, by two, that were cunning' (Hertford 1591 f E2v), and in 1613, Thomas Campion described the singing of an unnamed countertenor with the words '[a] Song was sung by an excellent countertenor voice, with rare varietie of division' (1613/3 f B1v). Fortunately for us today, the virtuoso embellishment style in use at that time has been captured in a number of manuscripts dating from the first quarter of the seventeenth century.[24] These manuscripts record the styles of embellishment used in England from ca 1610 to ca 1625, that is, the last fifteen or so years of John Dowland's life. The divisions and graces are applied to earlier songs (from the first decade of the century) as well as later ones (from the 1620s). My purpose, however, is not to concentrate on the embellishment style of any particular period during the first quarter of the seventeenth century but to expose the wide range of practices singers employed during these years.

Within these manuscripts, two distinct types of ornamentation are found – what I will call graces and divisions. Graces are small melodic figures, frequently of no more than a few notes, which embellish single notes of the original melody, and a number of these are indicated in the sources by stylized signs or are fully written out. Divisions, on the other hand, are longer figural patterns applied to several or many notes of the original melody, serving to divide longer notes into shorter ones, and numerous examples of these are completely written out in the manuscript sources.[25] Moreover, the manuscripts contain several different styles of ornamentation that, because of the dates of the sources, must have coexisted in the second and third decades of the century. The Turpyn songbook (ca 1610–15), for instance, reflects the earlier sixteenth-century division style as exemplified by Diego Ortiz (1553), but some of the other manuscripts, especially Tenbury 1018 and 1019 (both ca 1615), Trinity College F.5.13 (ca 1615), Egerton 2971 (second decade of the century), Add 24665 (ca 1615–ca 1626), Fitzwilliam Mu 782 (ca 1620), and Add 29481 (1620s), illustrate the later sixteenth-century Italian style of embellishment as exemplified by dalla Casa (1584), Bassano (1585 and 1591), Rogniono (1592), and Bovicelli (1594), as well as certain aspects of the styles of Notari (1613) and Rognioni (1620). The two manuscripts in the Christ Church Library (439 [before 1620] and 87 [ca 1624]), in addition to notating graces more frequently than other sources, seem to continue the Italian tradition.

DIVISIONS

One of the styles of ornamentation still employed in the second decade of the seventeenth century involved adding divisions to a vocal melody in the same way that musicians, such as the Spaniard Diego Ortiz (1553), would have done some sixty years earlier. Robert Parsons' song 'Poure downe you powers devyne' from the Turpyn songbook illustrates how this older technique was applied in England (see Ex 2.8).[26] Parsons died in 1570, and we do not know whether the Turpyn reading was newly created in the seventeenth century or whether it was simply a copy of a much earlier version of the song. Nevertheless, its existence in a manuscript copied

at some point between 1610 and 1615 does show that this style of ornamentation continued to be performed in the second decade of the century. The figures added to the melody are either identical to or similar to
those given by Ortiz in his embellishment tables, and the method of
applying these figural patterns in the Turpyn songbook simply was to
superimpose them on the vocal line, which allowed the original melody to
be easily discerned beneath the divisions – one of the hallmarks of the
embellishment style in vogue between ca 1530 and ca 1560.[27] Moreover,
the figuration is added only toward the ends of phrases, mainly at the
cadences themselves, and this makes these divisions excellent examples of
how one might ornament *clausulae* in a mid-sixteenth-century style. Their
elegant simplicity represents one end of the spectrum of vocal divisions,
for in both the sixteenth and the seventeenth centuries, divisions could be
much more complex and virtuosic than the Turpyn manuscript suggests.

More common in the second and third decades of the century was a
style of ornamentation in which divisions, predominantly in the form of
figures composed of semiquavers, were applied intermittently to an entire
song. In fact, with the exception of British Library, Add 15117 and the
Turpyn songbook, all of the manuscripts listed above contain pieces
embellished in this manner. However, as one would expect, a number of
different styles of division-making existed within this general approach.
Representative of one of these styles is a version of John Wilbye's 'Weepe
myne eyes' from Egerton 2971 (see Ex 2.9). The divisions applied to this
song replace longer notes of the original melody with shorter ones in a
style reminiscent of ornamentation found in Bassano (1585, 1591). Leaps
are filled in (bars 3, 7) and repeated notes are decorated by figures that
begin and end on the original note (bars 4, 10). At other times, the divisions stray quite far from the original melody (bar 9), and at the end of
the song, the final cadence is expanded through divisions which double
the lengths of the penultimate and antepenultimate notes. Although
cadences receive a considerable amount of decoration throughout the
song, the divisions by no means are restricted to *clausulae*, for they appear
at both the beginnings (bar 14) and middle portions (bars 5–7) of phrases.
Furthermore, some of the figures employ musical *climax* as a way of
increasing the forward drive, and thereby the intensity, of the figuration

Ex 2.8 'Poure downe you powers devyne'

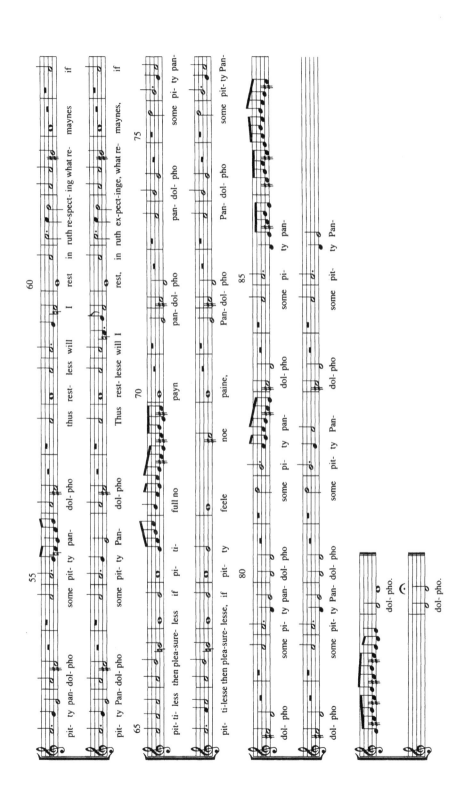

Ex 2.9 'Weepe myne eyes'

(bars 7, 10, 14). Interestingly, the ornamentation seems to have been conceived mainly for musical reasons, as unimportant words, such as 'and'
(bar 9), as well as rather more important words, such as 'no' (bar 4) and
'thousand' (bar 14), receive musical emphasis through divisions. All of the
above comments apply equally well to the three other songs in Egerton
2971 that were ornamented, the anonymous 'This merrie pleasant
springe' (f 16v) and 'Art thou that she' (f 9v), and Alfonso Ferrabosco's
'Drowne not with teares' (f 13v). One song in Christ Church 439,
Nathaniel Giles' 'O heare my prayer Lord' (p 64), is ornamented in a
similar manner. In fact, this non-textual approach may form part of what
John Dowland was referring to when he wrote of 'simple Cantors, or
vocall singers' and their 'blinde Division-making' (1612 'To the Reader').
This type of division-making certainly would destroy any carefully constructed connection between verbal and musical rhetoric.

Undoubtedly, Dowland also would have scorned a singer like Giles
Earle, owner of Add 24665,[28] because the divisions in his book easily
would have earned the contemptuous remark that such 'blinde Division-
making' was the product of a singer who was 'meerley ignorant, even in
the first elements of Musicke' (Dowland 1612 'To the Reader'). However,
in 1612, Dowland felt that he was considered old-fashioned. In reference
to the 'simple Cantors, or vocall singers,' Dowland laments 'yet doe these
fellowes give their verdict of me behinde my backe, and say, what I doe is
after the old manner' (1612 'To the Reader'). Taste in 'Division-making'
obviously was changing, and the version of Daniel Batchelar's 'To plead
my faith' in Earle's book (Ex 2.10), in addition to illustrating another of
the early seventeenth-century styles of ornamentation, may well contain
the type of divisions which Dowland's traditional musical temperament
could not abide. Nonetheless, on closer examination the divisions in 'To
plead my faith' really are not so blind; rather they exemplify one of the
approaches to embellishment that existed during the last decade of
Dowland's life. The art recorded by Giles Earle[29] was a sophisticated
one, and his version of 'To plead my faith' reveals the liberty with which
some singers incorporated divisions.

In contrast to singers represented in other manuscripts of the period,
Earle exhibited great rhythmic freedom in dividing longer notes into

shorter ones. He was not concerned with replacing minims, for example, with shorter notes that totalled the same rhythmic value as the original note, for sometimes he substituted more notes than the original time value strictly would allow (see bar 9 where the last minim is replaced by the equivalent of eleven semiquavers instead of the usual eight, as well as bars 31, 57, 59, 63 where similar procedures occur on minims). Like other singers, however, he frequently expanded the penultimate and/or antepenultimate notes of the original to accommodate elaborate cadential figuration (bars 11, 19, 23, 27, 31, 39). Not all cadences received this expansive treatment, however (bars 3–4, 7–8, 15–16, 35–6, 43–4, 47–8, 51–2, 55–6), and he occasionally employed this sort of elaborate figuration at the beginnings of phrases as well (bars 9 and especially 57). The specific figural patterns he uses are, nonetheless, typical of his time, sharing many traits with other sources, and similarly to 'Weepe myne eyes,' Earle's divisions seem to have been conceived for musical rather than textual reasons. Earle, too, fills in leaps (bar 5) and strays from the original melody, even in the simplest ornamentation (bar 14). He also creates, like the singer in Egerton 2971, the musical figure *climax* through his embellishments, using it to intensify the rising, stepward motion of the original melody (bar 29). The use of *climax* and *gradatio* (the extension of the figure beyond one restatement) is, of course, a common way of decorating scalar passages, and a number of examples can be found in both English and Italian sources (see Ex 2.11).

Four other manuscripts from about the same time period as Earle's songbook, Christ Church 439 (before 1620) and 87 (Elizabeth Davenant's songbook, ca 1624), Fitzwilliam Mu 782 (ca 1620),[30] and British Library, Add 29481 (1620s), show that the rhythmic freedom characteristic of some of the divisions in 'To plead my faith' was a common feature of vocal ornamentation. In Alfonso Ferrabosco's 'Why stayes the bridegroome' from Christ Church 439 (Ex 2.12), the rhythmic freedom is found near the beginning of the song (bar 3), and almost every cadence is expanded to carry elaborate ornamentation (bars 5, 10, 15, 23–4). Two songs by Thomas Campion illustrate the same principle, but to a lesser degree. Although 'Come you pretty false-ey'd wanton' from Elizabeth Davenant's songbook (Ex 2.13) receives rhythmic expansion in just one

Ex 2.10 'To plead my faith'

* One note has been added to make this cadential figure identical to that of bar 27.

Ex 2.11 Ascending and descending scalar passages

[Note the backfalls which take half the
value of the original note.]

Ex 2.12 'Why stayes the bridegroome'

Ex 2.13 'Come you pretty false-ey'd wanton'

place (bar 7),[31] the reading does demonstrate how a singer added divisions to an entire song in a more or less continuous manner. The second phrase is particularly instructive, for it shows a way of applying discrete figural patterns to about two-thirds of the notes while maintaining the contour of the original melody. 'Shall I come sweet love to thee' from Add 29481 (Ex 2.14) also contains just one passage in which rhythmic freedom is present (bars 10–11), and like the Turpyn songbook the divisions are confined to cadences. However, unlike the cadential treatment in Christ Church 439 and Giles Earle's songbook, the divisions remain within the context of the original melody, never increasing the overall length of cadential progressions (bars 3, 15, 21, 24).

A number of options for modern performers who wish to incorporate divisions in their own performances emerge from the surviving manuscripts. One might follow mid-sixteenth-century practices and ornament cadences with divisions similar to those found in Ortiz 1553 and the Turpyn songbook (Ex 2.8). Or one might apply discrete figuration to entire musical phrases in the manner suggested by Christ Church 87 (Ex 2.13). But if highly elaborate ornamentation is preferred, then one could model divisions on two practices. The rhythmic freedom and expansive treatment of cadences exhibited in Giles Earle's songbook would be one alternative (Ex 2.10), and the other possibility would be to follow the less flamboyant but still complex divisions of Egerton 2971 (Ex 2.9). Of course, one could decide not to add any divisions at all, and this, too, would be in keeping with historical precedent, for not every song in the manuscripts discussed here carries divisions.

GRACES

In addition to providing a wealth of information on divisions, a number of the manuscripts document the use of graces in the second and third decades of the century. Fortunately, many of the graces in these sources are written out in full, and this allows us to achieve a reasonably secure interpretation of the stylized signs that appear in the manuscripts. The graces commonly used in England during this period remained in vogue for much of the century, as later sources confirm, and often are identical

Ex 2.14 'Shall I come sweet love to thee'

to ornaments found in late sixteenth- and early seventeenth-century Italian sources. The written-out graces include the shake, relish, cadent, elevation or fall, backfall, and springer, whereas the stylized signs include the shake, cadent, elevation, springer, and beate. The signs and their interpretation, as derived from various later seventeenth-century English sources, appear in Table 2.2.[32] This table agrees, for the most part, with the written-out graces that are notated in both the English song manuscripts under discussion and the Italian sources listed in the preceding section (see Table 2.3).

The shake is written out as a cadential ornament in several places in the English song manuscripts (1-b in Table 2.3) and is used to depict the word 'quiver' in all three sources that contain 'This merry pleasant spring' (the Turpyn songbook, Egerton 2971, and Christ Church 439) (1-a). Although I have not found identical passages in Italian sources, dalla Casa's cadential ornamentation is quite similar (1-c, d). The relish occurs only in Christ Church 87 but not in the form described in later seventeenth-century sources; rather it conforms to Thomas Robinson's (1603) explanation of the grace as an upper-note figure (2). Both English and Italian sources notate the cadent in an identical fashion (3-a, b, d, e), the earliest example of the fully written-out grace in the English song manuscripts discussed here coming from the Turpyn songbook (3-c). Elevations or falls, however, occur in a wide variety of forms. The most common configuration in English sources is that shown in 4-a, b, where the grace is applied to long as well as short notes, but the elevation also appears in the form given in 4-c. Moreover, elevations sometimes are extended beyond the interval of a third to encompass a fourth (4-d), fifth (4-e), or even an octave (4-f). Yet quite a different type of elevation, the dotted form, is shared between English and Italian sources (4-g to k). Although in 4-g it is not clear whether the grace is to be performed before the beat or on the beat, 4-h shows that the ornament is meant to start on the beat (as the sources in Table 2.2 illustrate) and takes time away from the note which is being ornamented. Italian sources confirm this reading (4-i, j), but before-the-beat interpretations do exist (4-k). Backfalls are present in two forms: the single (5-a, b) and the double (5-c to e). In the one English source which writes out a single backfall, Christ

Table 2.2 Graces from later seventeenth-century English sources

Shake		Simpson & Playford [derived from the close shake] Manchester & Mace = .a
Beate		Simpson & Playford
Beate shaked		Simpson & Playford
Fall	×d acd	Manchester & Mace [wholefall for Mace]
Halfefall	∕f e f	Mace
Backfall		Simpson, Playford, & Mace
Backfall shaked		Simpson, Playford, & Mace
Double Backfall		Simpson, Playford, & Manchester
Relish	℃⌐ cac	Manchester & Mace [Mace = ∴] Note: Robinson 1603 = cdc
Relish with backfall	ꝯc dcac	Manchester
Elevation		Simpson, Playford, & Manchester
Cadent		Simpson & Playford
Springer		Simpson & Playford

Sources: Manchester. Public Library, Watson Collection, ms 832 Vu 51[ca 1660]
Simpson, Christopher. The Division-Viol. London 1665
Playford, John. An Introduction to the Skill of Musick. London 1674
Mace, Thomas. Musick's Monument. London 1676

Church 439 (5-a), the grace note appears to be of short duration in relation to the main note (as the later sources in Table 2.2 indicate), but in one of the Italian sources, Rognioni 1620 (5-b), both the grace note and the main note are of the same duration. Interestingly, it is the same English source, Christ Church 439, which provides examples of written-out double backfalls. In 5-c, the ornament clearly is to be performed before the beat (in opposition to the later English sources shown in Table 2.2), and this interpretation is supported by at least one Italian source (5-d), but in 5-e, the grace is performed on the beat. The final grace to be discussed, the springer, occurs in Tenbury 1018, where it is used in a series to decorate a descending melodic line (6-a), and this grace also appears in Italian sources, especially Bovicelli 1594 (6-b).

In addition to writing out a number of graces in full, the manuscripts use stylized signs to indicate five ornaments (see Table 2.4). If the graces are viewed in relation to Tables 2.2 and 2.3, the realization of these signs presents only one problem. The primary difficulty concerns whether the shake should begin on the main note or its upper neighbour. This is especially problematic when the note to receive the shake is preceded by the upper neighbour (Table 2.4, 1-a to c). It may be perfectly within the bounds of normal practices, therefore, to begin the shake with a backfall (see Table 2.2, backfall and shake). For this reason, I have suggested two solutions for each example. But without knowing the precise configuration of the ornament the copyist was intending to suggest by his sign, all solutions must remain speculative.

The interpretation of two of the signs in Table 2.4 (♩ & ♪) has been aided by Edward Bevin's table of ornaments entitled 'Graces in play' in the keyboard manuscript British Library, Add 31403 (f 5r; see Ex 2.15). David Wulstan (1985 pp 130–1) argues that Bevin's table belongs to the second quarter of the seventeenth century and that because the section of Add 31403 that Bevin copied contains works by Bull, Gibbons, Byrd, and others, the signs may reflect earlier practices. Wulstan's hypothesis is probably correct, for it is corroborated by written-out graces in both the English and Italian vocal sources discussed above. It would appear, then, that singers and keyboard players employed some of the same graces. Moreover, the hook at the right end of the second stroke in bar 1 seems to

Table 2.3 Written-out graces

Table 2.4 Grace signs

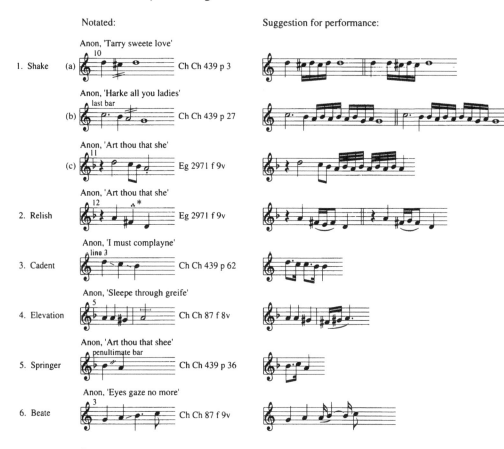

*
Sign appears in Table 2.2 under relish (Mace).

instruct performers to conclude the grace with a backfall, whereas the hook at the left end of the double stroke in bar 2 probably indicates that the shake should begin with a backfall, that is, should begin on the upper note.

Ex 2.15 'Graces in play'

In the song manuscripts, graces frequently are accompanied by divisions, and Alfonso Ferrabosco's 'Why stayes the bridegroome' from Christ Church 439 (Ex 2.12) provides an excellent example of how singers in the second decade of the century combined graces and divisions to create a highly ornate reading of a lute-song. Almost half of the notes are embellished in one way or another, the style of ornamentation extending from single-note graces to elaborate divisions which expand cadential passages. Elevations abound (bars 1, 3, 7, 9, 13, 14, 17, 18, 20, 21) and both single (bars 14, 19) and double (bars 1, 18) backfalls appear. At one point (bar 15), where the notes of the original melody are slurred together, the singer can produce the effect of a backfall occurring before the beat simply by observing the slurs. And in typical early seventeenth-century fashion, each main cadence (bars 5–6, 10–11, 15–16, 23–4) is expanded through divisions, the most elaborate decoration being saved for the final cadence.

The ability to add graces and divisions to songs obviously was a highly desirable skill for seventeenth-century singers to attain, and undoubtedly modern singers should gain this facility as well. But the question we must ask ourselves today in relation to ornamentation is 'Just how "blind" should our divisions and graces actually be?' In other words, which historical model(s) should we follow? I make no specific recommendations except to point out that singing without ornaments, singing with embellishments which do not alter the basic structure of the song, as well as singing with highly elaborate figuration find precedence in historical documents.

⁘ *To Act Aptly*

The art of speaking and singing well, as outlined in the preceding sections, could not reach perfection, of course, if it lacked action. Thomas Heywood maintained that without action the other parts of oratory (invention, disposition, elocution, memory, and even pronunciation) remain imperfect.[33] The orator's invention never would be so fluent and exquisite, his disposition and order never so composed and formal, his eloquence and elaborate phrases never so material and pithy, his memory never so firm and retentive, and his pronunciation never so musical and plausive if it is void of 'a comely and elegant gesture, a gratious and a bewitching kinde of action, a naturall and familiar motion of the head, the hand, the body, and a moderate and fit countenance sutable to all the rest' (1612 f c4r). Heywood, in addition to stressing how important action involving the head, hand, and body is to speaking, tells us about the way in which *elocutio* and *pronunciatio* are interrelated: 'It [and here Heywood refers to the value of rhetoric for young scholars] instructs him to fit his phrases [*elocutio*] to his action, and his action to his phrase, and his pronuntiation to them both' (1612 f c4r). Clearly then, action, as well as the other aspects of delivery, must match the text. Thomas Wright (1604 p 124) takes our understanding of action one step further, suggesting that the internal conceits and affections of the mind are expressed not only with words but also with actions, the two vehicles through which the orator penetrates the ears and eyes of listeners thus gaining access to their souls. For this reason, he states, rhetoricians are not content with a simple pronunciation of their orations. They enhance their discourse by prescribing many rules of action, and this enables them to imprint affections much deeper in the souls of listeners. Both words and actions, he concludes, spring from the same root, that is, understanding and affections. We are reminded, once again, of the importance of gaining a knowledge of the rhetorical structure of texts and the passions which are embodied in those texts, for our style of delivery will be shaped by a detailed understanding of the text.

It seems likely that at least some singers in early seventeenth-century England aligned themselves with orators and graced their delivery with action, for Philip Rosseter, in defending the simple, 'naked' ayre against its detractors, speaks to the subject directly. He asserts that the childish sort of action exploited in Comedies should be avoided, stressing that a 'manly cariage,' both in setting words to notes and in reinforcing words with action, should be maintained: 'But there are some [musicians], who to appear the more deepe, and singular in their judgement, will admit no Musicke but that which is long, intricate, bated with fuge, chaind with sincopation, and where the nature of everie word is precisely exprest in the Note, like the old exploded action in Comedies, when if they did pronounce *Memeni*, they would point to the hinder part of their heads, if *Video*, put their finger in their eye. But such childish observing of words is altogether ridiculous, and we [musicians in Rosseter's day, that is, composers and singers] ought to maintaine as well in Notes, as in action a manly cariage, gracing no word, but that which is eminent, and emphaticall' (1601 'To the Reader'). Rosseter's attitude toward gesture dates back to at least the time of Quintilian, for Quintilian condemns those who use the hands to illustrate anything they may chance to say (xi pp 290–1). Rosseter is, of course, expressing an informed opinion, and his interest in the theatrical world manifests itself during the years 1609–17, when he was one of the theatrical managers for the Children of Blackfriars, later called the Children of the Queen's Revels.[34]

Although Rosseter's tantalizingly short reference to action in singing, the only reference known to me from English sources of this period, does not tell us exactly what gestures should replace childish action, Rosseter's notions about gesture are echoed and amplified by other English writers on the subject. Abraham Fraunce, for example, frames his opening remarks on action in a remarkably similar fashion: 'The gesture must followe the change and varietie of the voyce, answering thereunto in everie respect: yet not so parasiticallie as stage plaiers use, but gravelie and decentlie as becommeth men of greater calling. Let the bodie therefore with a manlike and grave motion of his sides rather followe the sentence than expresse everie particular word' (1588 II chap 3). And John Bulwer maintains that even though 'gesture must attend upon every flexion of the voice,' it should not be demonstrated scenically (1644 p 241). Moreover, Rosseter's example of parasitic action on words like *memeni* and *video* would find a place in Fraunce's description quite easily, for Fraunce suggests that action simply follow the sentence. It seems to me that the two writers, Rosseter and Fraunce, are implying the same thing. By selecting only the most important word in a phrase or sentence, a word which may embody the affection expressed in the entire sentence or phrase, one would, in fact, derive action from those 'eminent and emphaticall' words which determine the character of the sentence.

We glean from Rosseter and Fraunce that a 'manly cariage' is as appropriate for oration as it is for singing. It would seem, then, that in England the singing of ayres was more akin to oration than it was to acting, and treatises on oration form a natural source from which to draw information on action in singing. Furthermore, musicians in other countries certainly were expected to be skilled in action, for in 1600 Emilio de' Cavalieri wrote that the singer should accompany the words with gestures (1600 preface). And some twenty years later, Marin Mersenne wrote of singers in France: 'Motum corporis, vultum praesertim, & manum cantui conformare debent, alioquin musica imperfecta, atque manca erit' / 'Singers must adapt the movement of the body, especially face and hand, [to the poetry,] otherwise the music will be imperfect and incomplete' (1623 col 1615; cited in Barnett 1987 p 17).

The most useful English sources which discuss the art of gesture are those by Fraunce (1588) and Bulwer (1644), with information from Le Faucheur (1657) supplementing and corroborating the two earlier writers. Fraunce gives particularly detailed information about the motion of the head, and Bulwer provides a wealth of information on the hands and fingers, mentioning no less than 87 separate gestures, together with 137 other types of directions, and illustrating all of this with numerous drawings of the hands and fingers. These writers, as well as others, suggest that action must be adapted to the voice, for gesture enriches the delivery by appealing to the eye in the same way that the voice speaks to the ear (Quintilian XI pp 250–1, Wilson 1553 p 437, Wright 1604 p 176, Bulwer 1644 p 5). Abraham Fraunce even goes so far as to recommend following the 'change and varietie of the voyce' in every respect.[35] Based on this, we, today, in preparing to deliver a song, probably should determine the disposition of the voice first so that we will know which sorts of gestures will enhance delivery in the most effective way. The previous sections have documented the options open to performers concerning the voice, and now we must turn our attention to the action of the whole body.

General advice is not hard to find. All action, it seems, begins with a natural imitation of the person who is to be impersonated: 'Qualifie every thing [that is, every gesture] according to the nature of the person personated' (Heywood 1612 f c4r). Thomas Wright, in fact, recommends careful observation of real life, for those who imitate best, act best: 'Looke upon other men appassionate, how they demeane themselves in passions, and observe what and how they speake in mirth, sadnesse, ire, feare, hope, &c, what motions are stirring in the eyes, hands, bodie, &c' (1604 p 179). Action, then, should reflect everyday life. Gestures never were frozen positions to be assumed at certain points in sentences but rather were fluid motions of the hands, fingers, head, and so on born from the thoughts and emotions that produce the words to be spoken. Action should be, to borrow the words of Thomas Wright, an external image of the passion in the mind (1604 p 179). But not all nations displayed the same temperament for action. According to John Bulwer, the Italians used too much gesture of the hand, and French action was full of 'quick and lightsome expressions.' But in Germany and England, countries with similar national complexions, 'moderation and gravity in gesture is esteemed the greater virtue.' The Spaniards, however, although equally disposed to moderate and grave action, use the hands 'as often [as] principals as accessories to their proud expressions' (1644 p 250). References to moderation and gravity permeate English writings on action. Thomas Wright, as quoted above, certainly advises orators to study 'other men appassionate' but recommends that they 'leave the excesse and exorbitant levitie or other defects, and keepe the manner corrected with prudent mediocritie' (1604 p 179). Fraunce and Rosseter employ words such as 'grave' and 'manly cariage' to describe the ideal approach to action (see above), and Bulwer, in recognizing national differences in temperament, advocates moderation in gesture, the golden mean being the best prescription for action (1644 p 249).

The art of gesture was to be studied assiduously, Bulwer and Le Faucheur suggesting practising before a mirror (Bulwer 1644 p 247, Le Faucheur 1657 p 175). In learning action, however, one should imitate only the best orators and perfect the techniques through exercise: 'Bend and wrest your arm and hands to the right, to the left, and to every part, that having made them obedient unto you, upon a sudden and the least signification of the mind you may show the glittering orbs of heaven and the gaping jaws of earth ... [so that] you may be ready for all variety of speech' (Bulwer 1644 pp 246–7). Gesture should, of course, be planned in advance, the speaker/singer determining beforehand the types of action which will be accommodated to the variety of the voice and the words. In preparation for applying action to a text, one should analyse the text, following the simple formula I have adapted from John Bulwer (1644 p 244). First, take note of the dominant passion. Next observe how the main parts of the text relate to this central emotion. Then study individual sentences to determine the specific affections embodied in them. Finally, decide which words in those sentences need to be emphasized through gesture. But we today should remember that John Bulwer also stressed that it was absurd to change gesture frequently in the same sentence. Once the requirements of the text were understood, orators and singers of the time could turn to treatises on action to find detailed prescriptions for specific motions which would give them, to use Thomas Wright's phraseology (1604 p 176), that visible eloquence of the body so necessary for the affection to pour forth by all means possible.

The 'comely grace' to which Wright and other writers refer concerned the whole body, that is, the stance of the orator as well as motions of the head, eyes, eyebrows, shoulders, arms, hands, fingers, and feet. In general, one should stand upright and straight, 'as nature hath appoynted,' without wavering about (Fraunce 1588 f J3v), for to change place and posture frequently was considered ridiculous. Nonetheless, one should 'neither *stand* like a *Stock*, nor be as immoveable as a *May-pole*' (Le Faucheur 1657 p 179). In fact, Fraunce considered it tolerable 'to stirre a step or two' as long as this movement was seldom, the place was large, and the auditors were numerous (1588 f K4v). The head should retain its natural position (modestly upright), departing from this to enhance the expression of a particular affection. For example, Fraunce comments that shaking the head denotes grief and indignation as well as compassion and that a nod is a token of a grant (1588 f K1r). But in order to show certain affections, Fraunce recommends combining the motion of the head with movement in the eyes, the eyes being the 'chiefest force' in the countenance. Modesty, he states, is best depicted by holding the head down while casting the eyes in the same direction (1588 ff J4r, K1r). Fraunce says little else about the eyes and nothing about the other parts of the face except that 'the particular ordering is left to everie mans discretion' (1588 f K2r).

Fortunately, Le Faucheur describes many of the motions to which Fraunce merely alludes. To depict anger, a fire must be seen in the eyes that makes them sparkle (1657 p 184). Violent grief, on the other hand, should draw tears from the eyes. Ancient actors, Le Faucheur contends, acquired the ability to counterfeit the '*Power* of *Weeping* and *shedding Tears*' in such abundance that when they left the stage their faces were 'all over blurr'd with *Crying*.' The method of producing tears he suggests involved keeping the imagination on real subjects and one's own private afflictions rather than on the '*Fables* or *Fictions* of the *Play*' to be acted. Moreover, Le Faucheur asserts that tears are as appropriate for the pulpit as they are for the stage (1657 pp 185, 188–9). One should lift up or cast down the eyes according to the subject matter. When speaking of heaven and celestial powers, look up, but when referring to earth and terrestrial things, look down. Similarly, in honour one should look up, whereas in disgrace one should look down (1657 p 191). The eyebrows should be contracted into a frown in sorrow, and one might dilate and smooth them in joy. They should be hung down, however, in humility and modesty (1657 p 192). For certain powerful affections, such as detestation and abhorrence, the motion of the head should be accompanied by action in the hands. Both Bulwer and Le Faucheur recommend similar gestures for these passionate rejections.[36] Bulwer suggests thrusting the left hand forward with the palm turned out, the left shoulder raised, and the head turned to the right as a way of repelling distasteful objects. But this action can be made even more passionate, he contends, if both hands are thrust out to the left side (1644 pp 186–7). For Le Faucheur, however, one rejects with the right hand, turning the head away to the left (1657 p 181).

The hand is, of course, the most powerful gesticulatory agent available to orators and singers. Both Bulwer (1644 p 239) and Le Faucheur (1657 p 194) refer to it as the 'chief instrument' of action, and Fraunce (1588 f K3r) maintains that, without the hand, gesture is nothing. The casting out of the arm and the hand allows speach 'to powre forth' and gives the figures contained in the text all the force, vigour, and efficacy that they require (Fraunce 1588 f K2r, Le Faucheur 1657 pp 199–200). The hands were to be used in certain prescribed ways, however, and the three sources which form the basis for my discussion generally agree with one another on the rules of action which apply to the hand. Bulwer's extraordinarily detailed descriptions of the hands dominates my treatment of the subject, for his book is by far the most thorough English account of hand gesture to survive from the first half of the seventeenth century. The main vehicle for gesture was the right hand, the left hand being used as an accessory rather than a principal in action. In fact, Bulwer notes that the left hand received its name because it usually was 'left' out (1644 p 234). Nonetheless, Bulwer did admit that the left hand could be used alone, but its normal role, if employed at all, was to accompany the right hand, for when the hands were used together, they were capable of exhibiting much more affection (1644 pp 247–8). The left hand was, however, never to be lifted as high as the right (Le Faucheur 1657 pp 196–7). In fact, the hands and arms operated within a carefully defined physical space. The hand is not to be raised above the eyes or to fall below the breast, and the arms should not be stretched out sideways more than half a foot from the trunk of the body. Consequently, the hands always are kept in view of the eyes, and their action consists of the following: motions to the right, to the left, up, down, and forward. Rhetoricians are not allowed backward or circular motions. Furthermore, gestures normally should pass from the left side of the body to the right and end on the right (Bulwer 1644 pp 240–1, Le Faucheur 1657 pp 198, 200–1).

It seems, based on the divergent opinions of the two English writers Fraunce and Bulwer, that gesture could either anticipate, accompany, or follow the words. For Bulwer, speech and gesture are conceived simultaneously in the mind, yet in delivery the hand appears first, giving shape to the thought before the words can complete it. In this way, action anticipates the words which both accompany and follow specific gestures. The addition of the words serves as a comment on and fuller explication of the gesture and is so necessary for a perfect understanding of action (1644 p 17). Fraunce, however, maintained that hand gesture should follow rather than go before the words (1588 f K3r), and this view is held by Le Faucheur as well, who emphasized that one should not begin with gesture and that action of the hand should be completed before one finishes speaking (1657 pp 198–9). On this last point, Bulwer seems to agree with Le Faucheur's contention that the hand should, so to speak, rise and fall with the sentence: 'When the oration begins to wax hot and prevelent, the hand may be put forth with a sentence but must withdraw again with the same' (1644 p 240). Within the discourse one should shun similitude of gesture, for this is akin to a monotone in the voice (Bulwer 1644 p 243). But do not use so much action that the hands are perpetually in motion (Bulwer 1644 p 224, Le Faucheur 1657 pp 201–2). The hands may, in fact, be idle for a time when no affection is emergent, but long intermissions are displeasing (Bulwer 1644 p 248). Bulwer suggests keeping silences in the hand to intervals of, perhaps, three words (1644 p 241). This undoubtedly would prevent one from changing gesture within a sentence too frequently (1644 p 241). And certainly at the beginning of a discourse do not start abruptly with the hand unless, of course, such action is warranted (Bulwer 1644 p 240, Le Faucheur 1657 p 195). Rather, the hand should break into gesture only after it is brought forward softly, Bulwer considering this stretching forth of the hand to be a posture of preparation (1644 pp 173, 240; illustrated in plate 3 C, E).

After being prepared, the hand could be used to heighten the passionate language of the text in a wide variety of ways. Bulwer describes dozens of specific postures for the hands and fingers, providing drawings for many of them (plates 1–5). These actions were to accompany the affections present in the text, and although most of the descriptions apply to individual passions, certain gestures were of a more general nature and were used to increase the vehemency of many different affections. Bulwer, in fact, considers eight separate gestures appropriate for this latter purpose and illustrates the five postures for the fingers with drawings. In order to grace any matter with a loftier style, the 'gentle and well ordered hand' should be 'thrown forth by a moderate projection, the fingers unfolding themselves in the motion and the shoulders a little slackened' (p 174). Moreover, if one wishes to reinforce an emphatic declaration (asseveration), gently spread the hand on the stomach (p 179) or smite the hands together with a 'certain kind of gravity' (p 189). But when one needs to stimulate or excite the listeners more, bring the two middle fingers under the thumb to create an action that is 'instant and importunate' (p 199; plate 5 D). Similarly, an argument can be urged and instantly enforced if the left thumb is pressed down by the index of the right hand (p 200; plate 5 w). A particularly effective method of driving 'the point into the heads of the auditors' is to turn the extended right index down, while composing the rest of the fingers into a fist (p 202; plate 5 P).[37] This same posture of the hand becomes a forceful indicatory action capable of showing many things (useful for scolding and indicating grief) when the hand and arm are held in a horizontal position (p 201; plate 5 M). Bulwer illustrates two other techniques for using the right index finger to increase vehemency: with it, apprehend the middle joint of the left index (p 200; plate 5 I) or apprehend the upper joint of the left index, but in this last case, the next two fingers of the left hand should assume a slightly bowed position and the small finger scarcely should be bent at all (p 200; plate 5 H). As part of their general approach to gesticulation, orators even may wish to mark the punctuation of the text with

Plate 1

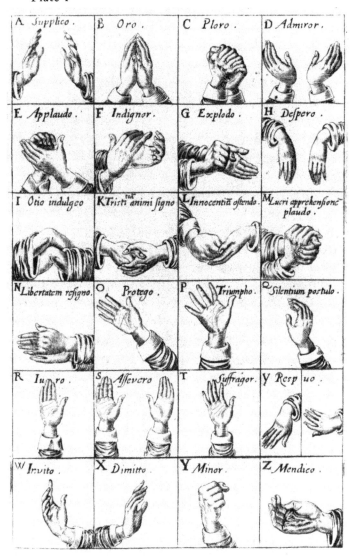

Bulwer 1644; reproduced by permission of the Syndics of Cambridge
University Library

A Entreat	G Explode	N Resign liberty	T Permit
B Pray	H Despair	O Protect	V Reject
C Weep	I Indulge in ease	P Triumph	W Invite
D Admire	K Mental anguish	Q Demand silence	X Dismiss
E Applaud	L Innocence	R Swear	Y Threaten
F Indignation	M Applaud the taking of money	S Declare emphatically	Z Beg

Plate 2

Bulwer 1644; reproduced by permission of the Syndics of Cambridge
University Library

A Reward	H Impede	O Adoration	T Reconcile
B Bring aid	I Recommend	P Affirm one's	V Suspicion and
C Anger	K Lead about	conscience	hate
D Show that one	L Betray	Q Display	W Honour
does not have	impatience	contrition	X Greet with
E Chastise	M Compel by	R Fear with	reservation
F Fight	repeated requests	indignation	Y Show thievery
G Confide	N Shame	S Pledge one's faith	Z Bless

Plate 3

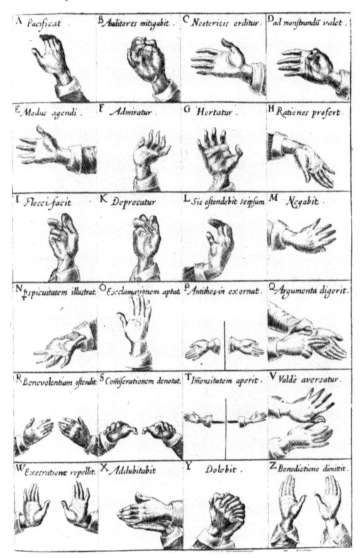

A *Pacificat.* B *Auditores mitigabit.* C *Neotericis orditur.* D *ad monstrandū valet.*
E *Modus agendi.* F *Admiratur.* G *Hortatur.* H *Rationes profert.*
I *Flocci facit.* K *Deprecatur.* L *Sic ostendebit seipsum.* M *Negabit.*
N *Pspicuitatem illustrat.* O *Exclamationem aptat.* P *Antithesin exornat.* Q *Argumenta digerit.*
R *Benevolentiam ostendit.* S *Comiserationem denotat.* T *Imensitatem aperit.* V *Valde aversatur.*
W *Execratione repellit.* X *Addubitabit.* Y *Dolebit.* Z *Benedictione dimittit.*

Bulwer 1644; reproduced by permission of the Syndics of Cambridge University Library

A Pacification
B Appease auditors
C Preparative gesture, convenient for exordium
D Show
E Preparative gesture
F Admiration
G Cheer, exhort
H Produce reasons
I Slight, undervalue
K Deprecate
L For speaking about oneself
M Abhor, repel
N Perspicuity
O Exclamation
P Antithesis
Q Digesting the arguments
R Benevolence
S Commiseration
T Show immensity
V More passionate detestation
W Extreme loathing
X Doubt
Y Grief, sorrow
Z Dismissal benediction

Plate 4

Bulwer 1644; reproduced by permission of the Syndics of Cambridge University Library

A Work in discovery
B Weep
C Approve
D Extol
E Show both sides
F Point
G Inflict terror

H Show silence
I Reprove
K Summon
L Disapprove
M Show hesitancy
N Betray weakness
O Provoke an argument

P Condemn
Q Impose irony
R Provoke contemptuously
S Betray avarice
T Resent a slight offence
V Betray mild anger

W Sign of folly
X Accuse of improbability
Y Give sparingly
Z Count

Plate 5

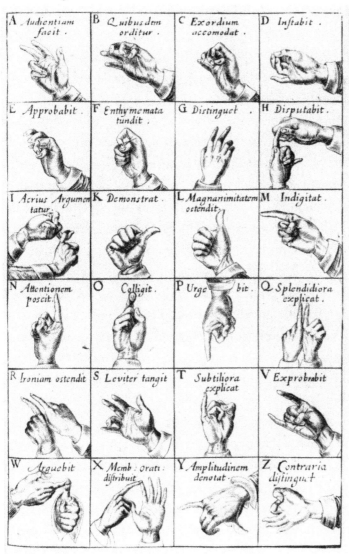

Bulwer 1644; reproduced by permission of the Syndics of Cambridge University Library

A Demand silence
B Hand fit for exordium
C Commodious for proem
D Urge
E Approve
F For enthymemes
G Show a small number
H Disputation
I For greater vehemence of a word
K Demonstration
L Magnanimity
M Forceful indication
N Threaten, denounce
O Confirm, refute
P Urge
Q Exaltation from splendid elocution
R Ironical intention
S For handling a matter lightly
T Explain subtle things
V Scoff, reproach
W Urge and instantly enforce an argument
X Number arguments
Y Denotes amplitude
Z To distinguish contraries

their hands. Bulwer suggests two procedures. Commas and the 'breathing parts of a sentence' may be distinguished with a 'gentle percussion, now greater, now less, now flat, now sharp, according to the diversity of the affections' (p 181). But for the 'close or period of a sentence' the hands may be 'gently set together by a sweet approach, causing a low sound by their light encounter or complosion' (p 188).

However, most action of the hand was designed to reinforce specific affections, and Bulwer's meticulous attention to detail allows us to recover with considerable accuracy the early seventeenth-century English art of coupling manual and verbal rhetoric. In treating Bulwer's prescriptions for artificially managing the hand, I will group the techniques according to affection, discussing related passions as a group. This arrangement of the material allows us to comprehend the subtle ways in which the elo quently ordered hand helped to produce a passionate style of delivery.

One of the largest groups of related affections encompasses grief, sorrow, sadness, despair, mental anguish, pity, and weeping. These affections, though similar, arise from such a wide variety of situations that a great number of hand gestures are needed to accommodate them. To apply the hand passionately to the head is a sign of anguish, sorrow, grief, impatiency, and lamentation, and brings action into line with the adage 'where there is sorrow, there is the finger' (p 71; plate 2 L). The beating of the head to which Bulwer refers serves to portray someone overcome with sorrow, as when a father learns that his son is dead. To strike the forehead with the hand, however, is an action of sadness particularly suited to great grief. Its effect is aided by weeping (pp 183–4).[38] Similarly, it is common to smite the thigh with the hand when one is enraged with grief. This gesture can, however, be used in fear, admiration, and amazement as well (pp 76–7; plate 2 R). The other English writer to discuss this gesture, Abraham Fraunce, also maintained that its employment was common but felt that it should be used to denote indignation (1588 f K4v). Furthermore, Fraunce suggests that 'vehemencie of speach' could be shown by striking the ground with the foot (1588 f K4v). When grief is deeply settled in the 'yearning bowels' and the style is sharp and inflamed, touch the breast with the ends of the fingers (Bulwer 1644 p 179). But when one wants to raise great motions in the minds of the auditors (grief, sorrow, repentance, and indignation) and draw tears from their eyes, strike the breast with an audible stroke (pp 74, 182–3; plate 2 Q, which gives the shape of the hand for smiting the breast). All of these motions are, of course, greatly enforced by tears. Tears are caused by sorrow, which itself is a product of contradictory spirits in the brain. Tears flow forth when this contradiction strains together the moisture of the brain and brings that moisture to the eyes. From this act of weeping follows the folding and hard wringing of the hands, one of the two gestures most appropriate for weeping and tears (pp 32–3; plate 1 C). The other gesture commonly used in crying is 'to put [one's] finger in the eye' in order to rub or wipe away the tears (pp 122–3; plate 4 B).

Despair, mental anguish, and pity are demonstrated with much gentler motions, however. To appear with fainting and dejected hands is a posture of, among other things,[39] utter despair (p 37; plate 1 H), and to hold the fingers inserted between each other demonstrates the mental anguish of those who have fallen into a 'melancholy muse' (p 39; plate 1 K). Pity is shown by extending and offering the right hand to someone (p 58) or by letting down the hand with the 'intent to rear some languishing creature from off the ground' (p 59). But both palms held averse before the breast denotes commiseration (p 189; plate 3 s).

A second broad category of related affections embraces those which are more menacing to listeners: anger, abhorrence, rejection, dismissal, condemnation, disapproval, threat, and terror. An expression of the hand frequently used to direct anger at a specific person involves showing and shaking the bended fist at that person (pp 52–3; plate 1 Y). To explode in anger, however, one should clap the right fist on the left palm often (p 36; plate 1 G). Similar violent motions, such as striking the table with the hand (p 59; plate 2 C) or the pulpit with the hand bent into a fist (p 182), accompany impatient anger and vehement contentions, and when the thigh is smitten with the hand, it is a sign of one fuming with indignation (p 185). Indignation could, nevertheless, also be demonstrated by suddenly smiting the left hand with the right (p 35; plate 1 F). Mild anger, however, is expressed with the fingers formed into a talon-like claw in order to scratch those who have provoked a 'cursed heart' (p 138; plate 4 v). Bulwer continues this last description by cautioning that this motion is 'no manly expression of the hand' and pertains more properly to children and vixens who are prone to wreak their despite upon others.

To shake the hand back and forth, with bent brows, is an action of abhorrence (p 181), and a resilient hand which leaps back to the left side of the body from where it descended makes an action suited to abomination (p 181). Detestation may be shown by holding up both hands with the palms adverse (p 187; plate 3 w), but a more passionate form of detestation may be demonstrated by turning out both palms and projecting them to the left side (p 187; plate 3 v). If, however, one simultaneously drove the palms out to either side, then the vehement effect of averseness would be doubled (p 187). In order to reject, negate, or repel some detestable thing, orators and singers may choose from at least three motions. First, the hand may be driven forward to the left at the same time that the left shoulder is brought forward and the head is inclined to the right (p 181). Second, while the head turns to the right, the left hand, with the palm turned backward, can thrust forth from a raised shoulder in an act of repulsion (pp 186–7; plate 3 M). Finally, one can wag the back part of the down-turned hand in a sudden, jerky movement or simply turn out the palm of the hand to form a natural expression of denial (pp 50–1; plate 1 v). Similarly, to wag and wave the hand, this time raised, with the palm turned out is a gesture of dismissal[40] (pp 51–2; plate 1 x), but to clap the hand suddenly on the breast denotes a chiding rebuke (p 182). Another subtler way of showing disapproval does exist, however: simply raise the hand and bow the index finger away from oneself (p 130; plate 4 L). But if one wished to condemn, slight, or insult, cast out the hand while snapping the middle finger sharply against the palm, causing an audible sound (p 134; plate 4 P).

Actions born from these sorts of denunciation border on those which threaten, and at least some hand gestures served both purposes. To direct the hand toward the auditors with an impetuous agitation of the arm not only denounces but also threatens (p 175), and to show and shake the clenched fist at the listeners does more than condemning and threatening; it strikes terror in them (pp 52–3; plate 1 Y). Similarly, the index finger raised from a fist and brandished in a menacing way denounces, threatens, and incites terror (pp 127, 202; plate 5 N).

An equally important but gentler group of related affections encompasses love, adoration, admiration, faith, honour, loyalty, modesty, exaltation, and joyful exclamation. A gentle stroke with the hand, that is, drawing the hand 'with a sweetening motion over the head or face of the party to whom we intend this insinuation,' signifies affectionate love (pp 66–7), and to press hard and wring another's hand is a natural expression of the amorous intentions of a lover who strives to imprint upon his mistress' hand a tacit hint of his affection[41] (p 93). But if one wished to express 'an incredible ardor of love lodged in his bosom and cleaving to his very marrow,' one would touch the breast with the ends of the fingers (p 179). A degree of courtly solemnity could be maintained in showing adoration, however, simply by kissing the hand or the forefinger. This sign of respect, Bulwer observes, is used frequently in the formalities of civil conversation (pp 73, 127–8; plate 2 o). Moreover, in order to dearly cherish those we love, put forth both hands in an embrace (p 96). Faith, honour, and loyalty are expressed by apprehending and kissing the back of another's hand (p 97; plate 2 w), whereas modesty is demonstrated by restraining and keeping in the hand[42] (p 175). A more extravagant form of showing admiration, particularly the type which borders on amazement and astonishment, would be, however, to throw up the hands to heaven (p 33; plate 1 d) or to strike the forehead with the hand[43] (pp 183–5). Another action convenient for admiration involves turning up the palm with the fingers joined together in preparation for reversing the position of the hand while spreading the fingers (p 177; plate 3 f). If admiration is taken one step further and becomes exaltation, put out the raised hand and shake it 'into a shout' (p 45; plate 1 p). However, a slightly less flamboyant way of amplifying one's joy or making a congratulatory exclamation simply would be to raise the hand aloft (p 177; plate 3 o). Yet the raised hand, especially when presented in a hollow manner and coupled with some sort of a grave motion of the wrist, could represent quite a different affection; that is, the act of raising the hand might cheer, exhort, embolden, or encourage (p 177; plate 3 g).

In addition to discussing the ways in which the hands could heighten the passions in the text, Bulwer identifies a number of gestures that allow orators to use action for other purposes.[44] For example, the hands may request or invite. Stretching out the hands requests, entreats, or solicits (p 21; plate 1 A), whereas putting forth the hand without any waving motion or beckoning with the hand invites or calls after (p 179). Furthermore, supplication, that is, entreatment, can be made more artificial if both hands are dejected (p 187). When orators or singers need to speak of themselves, they should refer the hand to their own bodies (p 181; plate 3 L), and to show contraries the turned-up hand should be transferred from the left side of the body to the right. Two finger postures are possible for this motion: while keeping the other fingers remiss, either bend in the thumb or join the top of the thumb to the middle of the nail of the index (pp 177–8, 200; see plate 5 z for a drawing of the latter posture of the fingers). Another equally effective way of showing antithesis or opposition, however, is to have both hands alternately 'behave themselves with equal art' in order to set off any matter (p 189).

Through the wide range of gesticulatory techniques that Bulwer and others describe, orators and singers in the early seventeenth century were able to convey their thoughts and passions to listeners with greater force and delight. The voice on its own could achieve a great deal, of course, but when the voice was augmented with action, delivery reached its most persuasive state. The purpose of delivery, as we already know, was to speak or sing eloquently and act aptly so that the minds of auditors could be captured and inflamed. The eyes and ears were the windows to the soul, and orators and singers drew upon a vast arsenal of skills to help them penetrate deeply into the soul, moving it to experience whatever passions the text they were delivering contained. I encourage singers today to acquire the same skills that early seventeenth-century singers possessed and to recreate that part of their culture which would allow us to place our intuitive emotional responses to the lute-song repertoire in a framework derived from the documents which transmit their culture to us. The principles of eloquent delivery, as discussed in this section, now may be applied to specific songs, and this will permit modern singers to emulate their seventeenth-century counterparts: 'Please the Eye, charm the Ear, and move the Passions.'

3 PASSIONATE AYRES PRONOUNCED

It was Henry Peacham the Younger who suggested the most compelling reason for applying principles derived from *elocutio* and *pronunciatio* to the lute-song repertoire of early seventeenth-century England. The passionate ayre, he proclaims, is a *prosopopoeia*,[1] and in the *prosopopoeia*, the singer feigns the affections and nature of the imaginary person in the text, using the techniques of delivery to place listeners in the same state of mind. Passionate ayres are particularly apt for demonstrating how we today might perform lute-songs, for these types of pieces are the most figurative of the genre and, therefore, are in the highest style. Figures copiously decorate these songs in the same way that they adorned the orator's discourse, and singers and orators made passionate ornaments manifest through voice and action. The purpose of figures, after all, is to help singers move and delight listeners, and if singers can learn to deliver passionate ayres well, then those songs in simpler, plainer styles should present few difficulties for modern performers. In fact, Thomas Campion, in his song 'When to her lute Corrina sings' (1601 no 6), elegantly captures the effect singers should have on their listeners:

> When to her lute Corrina sings,
> Her voice revives the leaden stringes,

And doth in highest noates appeare
As any challeng'd eccho cleere,
But when she doth of mourning speake,
Ev'n with her sighes the strings do breake.

And as her lute doth live or die,
Led by her passion, so must I,
For when of pleasure she doth sing,
My thoughts enjoy a sodaine spring,
But if she doth of sorrow speake,
Ev'n from my hart the strings doe breake.

Perhaps two of the most sublime and pithy expressions of the passionate ayre are John Dowland's 'Sorrow sorrow stay' (1600 no 3) and 'In
darknesse let mee dwell' (1610 no 10). These ayres are imbued with all of
the rhetorical artifice one would expect to find in a *prosopopoeia*, and a successful performance of them depends upon the singer's ability to feign
the affections in the texts and use the musical and rhetorical devices present in the songs to create the persuasive style of delivery they demand.
In preparing to perform these songs, I suggest that singers follow the
approach recommended in treatises of the period. First, consider the passions of the poem. Note the dominant affection and determine how the
main parts of the text relate to this central passion. Then study individual
sentences to discover the specific affections embodied in them. At the
same time, observe the figurative language with which sentences have
been decorated and decide which words require emphasis. Do not over-
look the punctuation, for it is the vehicle through which the structure of
the discourse is articulated, and the observance of it enables listeners to
comprehend the thoughts and emotions of the texts easily. At this point,
the study of the structure of the text should be complete. Next one would
decide how the poem should be pronounced, taking care to match voice
and gesture to the passions contained therein. This leads singers, of
course, to the very useful exercise of presenting the poem as a dramatic
reading, for as Thomas Campion says of the ayres in his first two books,
'Omnia nec nostris bona sunt, sed nec mala libris; si placet hac cantes, hac

quoque lege legas' / 'Not everything of ours in these books is good, but neither is it bad; by this rule, if it [the song] pleases, you may sing it, also you may read it aloud' (1613/1 'To the Reader'). When singers can deliver the poem convincingly in the spoken realm, the basis for delivering the poem as a song already has been established. Singers are now in a position to determine how much of the spoken delivery actually can be transferred to the song itself. To do this, the singer must consider the nature of the musical setting carefully. What rhetorical devices in the poem have been reinforced by melodic or harmonic figures? In what other ways does the music reflect the sentiments of the poem? How does the punctuation in the poem control musical phrasing and articulation? Remember that musical notation in late sixteenth- and early seventeenth-century England was not overly fussy. Subtleties of articulation and phrasing rarely were notated, and indications of tempo and dynamics never seem to have been written down by composers or performers. After studying the manner in which the composer set the poem to music, the singer can make the final decisions for delivering the poem as a song. The last stage in the process of preparing a song for performance, of course, is to commit the piece and its style of delivery to memory.

In order to demonstrate how all of this may be applied to the lute-song repertoire, I will discuss Dowland's 'Sorrow sorrow stay' and 'In darknesse let mee dwell' and show various ways in which singers might communicate the passionate sentiments of the poems to listeners, while rooting their interpretations in historical documents. The discussion will follow the approach outlined above, and because I firmly believe that careful study of the poem should precede singing, I treat the poetry first. But in doing so, I will concentrate only on those figures and passionate ornaments that speakers and singers actually need to make manifest through voice and gesture. However, even though I strongly advocate that singers should master the poem first, learning to read it aloud, I do not wish to labour the point; therefore, I will treat speaking and singing separately in only one of the songs, 'Sorrow sorrow stay.'

Both of the poems Dowland set belong to the form of persuasion known as pathos, the purpose of which is to arouse certain states of mind in the listener by appealing to the emotions that colour the judgment.

The generic name for figures whose function is the stirring of the affections is *pathopoeia*. Henry Peacham the Elder discusses this term:

> Pathopeia, is a forme of speech by which the Orator moveth the minds of his hearers to some vehemency of affection, as of indignation[,] feare, envy, hatred, hope, gladnesse, mirth[,] laughter, sadnesse or sorrow: of this there be two kindes. The first is when the Orator being moved himselfe with anie of these affections (sorrow excepted) doth bend & apply his speech to stir his hearers to the same: and this kinde is called Imagination ... The other kind of Pathopeia, is when the Orator by declaring some lamentable cause, moveth his hearers to pitie and compassion, to shew mercy, and to pardon offences ... A serious and deepe affection in the Orator is a mightie furtherance and helpe to this figure, as when he is zealous, and deeply touched himselfe with any of those vehement affections, but specially if he be inwardly moved with a pitifull affection, he moveth his hearers to the same compassion and pitie, by his passionate pronuntiation ... This figure pertaineth properly to move affections, which is a principall and singular vertue of eloquution. (1593 pp 143–5)

The poems of each song are given below, together with the words as set by Dowland.

'SORROW SORROW STAY'

Undecorated poem (reconstructed following the example of Coprario cited below):

Sorrow stay, lend true repentant teares,
    To a woefull wretched wight,
Hence, dispaire with thy tormenting feares:
    O doe not my poore heart affright,

Pitty, help now or never,
    Mark me not to endlesse paine,
Alas I am condempned ever,
    No hope, no help, ther doth remaine,
But downe, down, down, down I fall,
    And arise, I never shall.

Words as set by Dowland:[2]

Sorrow sorrow stay, lend true repentant teares,
    To a woefull, woefull wretched wight, [.]
Hence, hence dispaire with thy tormenting feares:
    Doe not, O doe not my heart poore heart affright, [.]
Pitty, pitty, pitty, pitty, pitty, pitty, help now or never,
    Mark me not to endlesse paine, mark me not
        to endlesse paine,
Alas I am condempne'd, alas I am condempne'd,
    I am condempned ever, [:]
    No hope, no help, ther doth remaine, [.]
But downe, down, down, down I fall,
But downe, down, down, down I fall,
    Downe and arise, downe and arise, I never shall, [.]
But downe, downe, downe[,] downe, I fall,
But downe, downe, downe[,] downe, I fall,
    Downe and arise, downe and arise, I never shall.

'IN DARKNESSE LET MEE DWELL'

Undecorated poem (as printed four years earlier in
Coprario 1606 no 4):

In darknesse let me dwell, the ground shall sorrow be,
The roofe despaire to barre all chearefull light from me,
The walles of marble black that moistned stil shall weepe,
My musicke hellish jarring sounds to banish frendly sleepe.

> Thus wedded to my woes, and bedded in my tombe,
> O let me dying live till death doth come.

Words as set by Dowland:

> In darknesse let mee dwell, The ground, the ground
>   shall sorrow, sorrow be,
> The roofe Dispaire to barre all, all cheerfull light
>   from mee,
> The wals of marble blacke that moistned, that moistned
>   still shall weepe, still shall weepe,
> My musicke, My musicke hellish, hellish jarring sounds,
>   jarring, jarring sounds to banish, banish
>   friendly sleepe.
> Thus wedded to my woes, And bedded to my Tombe,
> O Let me living die, O let me living, let me living,
>   living die, Till death, till death doe come, till
>   death, till death doe come, till death, till death
>   doe come,
> In darknesse let mee dwell.

In order to further the persuasive quality of the vehement affections expressed in the texts of the two songs, Dowland amplifies the basic structure of the poetry by creating figures not present in the poems. My discussion of the amplificatory devices in the two texts assumes that Dowland adapted pre-existing poems. But since the authorship of these poems is unknown, the possibility arises that Dowland may have penned these verses himself with the figures of repetition forming part of his original conception. This is unlikely, however, in the case of 'In darknesse let mee dwell.' As noted above, the same poem with a few variants was set to music four years earlier by John Coprario, and this might have been Dowland's source for the text. Interestingly, the complete poem, stripped of the few textual devices added by Coprario in his setting, is printed below the music. The inclusion of the unembellished text clearly demonstrates how both Coprario and Dowland employed rhetorical

figures to expand the basic structure of the poem. Although no undecorated model of 'Sorrow sorrow stay' is known to exist, it probably is safe
to assume that Dowland's text represents a version amplified by rhetorical
devices. Indeed, the expansion of a basic text seems to have been a procedure commonly employed by Dowland, for over half of his solo songs
augment the vehemency of persuasion through figures of repetition.
Dowland's frequent use of *epizeuxis* (the immediate restatement of a word
or phrase for greater vehemency), for example, embodies a compositional
decision to stress and thus elicit in the listener the state of mind associated with that word or phrase. Various passages in both texts exemplify
the procedure. At the opening of 'Sorrow sorrow stay,' the repetition of
the word 'sorrow' draws attention to and establishes the character of the
ruling passion. Later, the reiteration of 'pitty' reinforces this state of
mind and categorizes the poem as Peacham the Elder's second type of
pathopoeia. Similarly, the restatements of 'mark me not to endlesse paine,'
'alas I am condempned,' 'but downe, down, down, down I fall,' and
'downe and arise' emphasize the significance of these phrases.

Dowland's amplification of 'In darknesse let mee dwell,' in addition to
the pervasive use of *epizeuxis*, involves another figure of repetition. As
mentioned earlier, through *anadiplosis*, that is, the repetition of the last
word of one phrase at the beginning of the next, the lines

> The roofe Dispaire to barre all cheerfull light from mee
> The wals of marble blacke that moistned still shall weepe

become

> The roofe Dispaire to barre all, all cheerfull light
>   from mee
> The wals of marble blacke that moistned, that moistned
>   still shall weepe, still shall weepe.

But as one would expect of a composer who has mastered both musical
and verbal rhetoric, Dowland increases the artificiality of the poem he
adapts by other means as well. The device used by Dowland to end the

song is known as *epanalepsis:* a unit that begins and ends with the same expression. The words 'In darknesse let mee dwell' open and close the song and form a striking proposition to be considered at the beginning and to be remembered at the end. Moreover, he employs *anastrophe* (a preposterous ordering of words which runs contrary to normal speaking [Sherry 1550 p 31]) to change the word order of Coprario's poem from 'O let me dying live' to 'O let me living die,' thereby accentuating the underlying torment of the text.[3]

Undoubtedly, a knowledge of these devices will help singers effectively deliver these poems both as dramatic readings and as songs, and I now wish to consider each song separately, illustrating in the process how the principles outlined in *elocutio* and *pronunciatio* form the basis of both eloquent speaking and singing. My suggestions are not intended to be prescriptive, for the principles of eloquent speaking and singing may be applied in a wide variety of ways.

'Sorrow Sorrow Stay'

As I indicated before, the central passion in this poem is sorrow. The images invoked by the poet revolve around the concept of sorrow, and words like 'teares,' 'dispaire,' 'tormenting feares,' 'pitty,' and 'endlesse paine' condemn this 'woefull wretched wight' to a life without hope or help in which he falls steadily downward, never to rise again. The amplificatory devices mentioned above aid the singer in delivering the text of the song as spoken verse, and our knowledge of both voice and gesture will help us create a passionate delivery suitable to the affections of the poem. However, in this portion of my discussion I will concentrate on the voice, leaving gesture until I consider the song itself.

The tonal quality of the voice appropriate for someone in this state of mind (based on Table 2.1) might be described as doleful and grave. It is a voice 'fetcht from the bottome of the throate, groaning' which is interrupted with woeful exclamations, sometimes breaking off abruptly with a sob or a sigh. Dowland begins by immediately amplifying the concept of sorrow through *epizeuxis*, a figure in which the repeated word is to be delivered with a 'different sound,' pronouncing it 'far louder and stronger.' I suggest, however, that if a speaker consistently took the same approach to pronouncing *epizeuxis* each time it appeared in Dowland's text, delivery would become too predictable. At times, the speaker might very well wish to utter the repeated word louder and stronger, but at other times, altering the tone colour of the voice might be just as effective. At any rate, whatever the speaker's decision regarding the pronunciation of *epizeuxis* might be, the repeated word must receive some sort of emphasis, for without this emphasis the figure is meaningless. The repetitions of 'woefull' and 'hence,' therefore, should be emphasized but perhaps in a way different from the utterance of 'sorrow.' In the fourth line of the text, however, the repetition 'Doe not, O doe not' is a special case, for it combines *epizeuxis* with *ecphonesis.* The exclamatory 'O' which precedes the repetition of 'Doe not' calls for the speaker to deliver this word with a louder and a more passionate accent. These woeful exclamations, a characteristic feature of texts dealing with sorrow, become most passionate when they are separated from other parts of the sentence by a sob or a sigh (either before or after the expletive). In uttering the whole phrase, speakers might wish to align themselves with John Hart's method of delivering exclamatory outbursts: begin the phrase loudly, as the expletive demands, and end it with a lower volume. Similarly, the six iterations of 'pitty' draw attention to this word in a most vehement way and remind us that emphatic devices are designed to heighten the expression of the sentiment on each repetition of a word. In pronouncing this application of *epizeuxis*, one needs to decide whether the strongest utterance of 'pitty' should be reserved for the final statement of the word or whether some other combination of gradations in volume, alterations in the tonal quality of the voice, changes in speed of delivery, and so on would be just as effective in moving listeners to feel pity for the 'woefull wretched wight' the speaker is representing.

Repetitions of whole phrases serve the same purpose. For example, the line 'Alas I am condempne'd, alas I am condempne'd, I am condempned ever:' uses *epizeuxis* to lead listeners in a graduated way to the climactic assertion 'I am condempned ever.' Momentum is achieved through the pronunciation of the figure, the colon allowing the speaker to pause at the climax just before being driven to utter the conclusion of the thought 'No hope, no help, ther doth remaine.' The vehement effect of the ensuing descent into despair once again is augmented through *epizeuxis*, each repetition of the word 'down,' like the word 'pitty,' being punctuated by commas *(articulus)*. Varying the length of pause between repetitions will give the speaker ample opportunity to alter the sense of the word, if so desired, each time it is reiterated (mainly through changes in the tonal quality of the voice, volume, and speed of delivery). By the end of the period, the speaker has resigned himself to remain in the depths of despair, and the utterance of the words 'I never shall' might be calculated to capture the bleak reality of the situation. Undoubtedly, some experimentation will be required while singers learn to deliver the text of the song in a persuasive manner. But remember, practice was the key to success: repeat a sentence over and over until it can be pronounced 'according to *Art*' (Le Faucheur 1657 p 214).

Dowland's mastery of affective musical persuasion is revealed in his musical setting of this *prosopopoeia* (see Ex 3.1). He couples words and notes in such an artful way that one seems to complement the other almost perfectly, and this makes the singer's task so much easier. Dowland appropriately places the song in the transposed *protus* mode; that is, the vocal line is in the hypodorian mode transposed to G (the so-called G-minor mode). He divides the song into three large sections, and each section ends with a strong cadence on the final of the mode, the conclusiveness being reinforced by a raised third in the lute part (bars 1–10, 11–22, 22–6 [repeated in a slightly extended form]). These cadences are the musical equivalents of the *periodus* in language and mark the main resting points in the musical discourse. Dowland further subdivides these three periods into a number of commas and colons, these smaller members focusing the listener's attention on specific ideas and affections. Each member, of course, requires an individual approach to its delivery, and this leads me to consider the members separately.

Dowland begins the song in recitative style, supporting the voice with simple chords. He enhances the vehement effect of the text's *epizeuxis*

Ex 3.1 John Dowland, 'Sorrow sorrow stay' (1600 no 3)

Ex 3.1 *(continued)*

with musical *climax*, and the interaction of these two figures colours my approach to delivering the proposition to be considered: 'Sorrow sorrow stay.' A slow arpeggiation of the opening G-minor chord invites the singer to implore sorrow to stay and hints at the grave subject matter that follows, for which the singer probably should adopt a doleful tonal quality in the voice. Dowland's melody, a descending two-note figure (rhythmically long-short), allows the singer to adapt one of the devices Giulio Caccini mentions as an important method of moving the affections of listeners; that is, crescendo on the first note of the figure and diminuendo on the second note.[4] On the repetition of the word 'sorrow' and its corresponding musical figure, the crescendo might be even more exaggerated in order to conform to the normal delivery of *epizeuxis* in which the repeated word is spoken with a louder voice. Moreover, a particularly poignant effect can be created if the singer reaches the peak of the first crescendo at the same time that the lutenist, in arpeggiating the chord below, plays the highest note of that chord (A), thereby accentuating the dissonance B♭/A. In the repetition of the figure, the same effect can be achieved between the singer's A and the lutenist's B♭.

The hand, of course, should reinforce the passionate appeal of the voice. When executed in a natural and unaffected manner (as opposed to the statue-like poses some singers adopt today), gesture should not seem strange or archaic to modern audiences. In fact, if one takes the advice of Thomas Wright seriously and observes people 'appassionate' in our own age, then one soon discovers that early seventeenth-century gesture really is not very far removed from current practices. Action based on historical principles will and does, I believe, reinforce the passions of the text in the same sort of realistic way that Wright, Rosseter, and others described. Several gestures are appropriate for the opening of the song, and Thomas Hobbes comments on the use of action to enhance figures of repetition: 'But in *Pleadings* [that is, orations to the people as distinct from judicial pleading], by the helpe of Action and by some change [of voice] in the *Pleader*, Repetition becomes Amplification' (1637 p 118). From its resting point in front of the chest, the hand might be brought forward softly as an act of preparation (Bulwer 1644; plate 3 c, ε). This preparatory gesture would then be transformed into the posture for sorrow and grief (plate 3 Y) at the moment the first 'sorrow' is uttered. But the final word of the proposition, depending on the singer's interpretation of the text, might be graced in more than one way. The hand could invite sorrow to stay (plate 1 W), it could beg it to stay (plate 1 Z), or it could command it to stay (plate 5 M). The singer may wish, however, to dispense with the preparatory gesture, preferring to create a more vehement effect at the outset by beginning abruptly with the posture for sorrow and grief. The only melodic ornamentation I would suggest for this passage, if one wished to add any at all, would be an elevation to the first note of the melody encompassing the interval of a third. This elevation probably should be duplicated for the repeat of 'sorrow' in order to preserve the integrity of the musical figure Dowland composed.

After the singer and lutenist deliver this rather arrresting *propositio* in a very free manner, a slow tempo, one which parallels the grave and doleful tonal quality of the voice that the text demands (perhaps a crotchet = 80–88), is established by the lutenist through the dotted figure which begins just as the singer finishes delivering the initial statement of the poem. The next textual phrase ('lend true repentant teares, to a woefull, woefull wretched wight') could be graced with purely melodic embellish-ments and with action that amplifies the underlying sentiments of the words. Specifically, singers might borrow from Christ Church 439, a manuscript which preserves the song only up to the first iteration of 'woefull,' the under-third elevations on 'lend' and 'pen' of 'repentant.' The meaning of the words, however, might be reinforced by three sepa-rate hand gestures. The torment of the singer can be shown in conjunc-tion with the words 'lend true repentant teares' through the posture for mental anguish (plate 1 K), and the repetition of 'woefull,' in addition to being emphasized by pronouncing the comma, may be stressed by one of the finger positions for urging an argument (for example, plate 5 D). This latter gesture would be transformed into the posture for speaking about oneself (plate 3 L) on the words 'wretched wight,' the hand returning to the resting position before one finishes singing 'wight.' The lutenist draws the period to a close, and the cadence at the beginning of bar 7 probably should be observed through a clear, but short, pause after the cadence note.

Dowland follows the punctuation of the text quite closely in the second period. Rests are composed into the melody for the commas at 'hence' and 'doe not,' and the colon at 'feares' is represented by a cadence on the fifth above the final of the mode, and this gives the musical expectation that much more is to be spoken. In fact, the lutenist pushes the song forward at this point with a new figure which leads the singer to an exclamatory outburst. The music written for the exclamation, the melodic equivalent of John Hart's loud beginning and soft ending, brings the first large section of the piece to a full and perfect close on the final of the mode (with a raised third in the lute part). The repetition of 'hence' at the beginning of this period might be enforced by uttering it with more intensity in order to prepare for an emphatic assertion of 'dispaire,' and 'dispaire' itself may be shown with fainting and dejected hands (plate 1 H). I suggest that the expletive 'O' be delivered in the Italian tradition with an *esclamazione*, specifically, by a quick decrescendo followed by a rapid crescendo.[5] This will create the emotional outburst which is intended, and the passionate force of the expletive will be increased if the hand is raised aloft (plate 3 O). In this case, one might leave the hand extended until near the end of the sentence, returning it to the resting position at the cadence. At this cadence, the singer should make a lengthy pause to give listeners enough time to reflect upon the entire text delivered to this point. And it is at the cadences ('feares' and 'affright') that melodic embellishments, perhaps in the form of discrete figures that would not obscure Dowland's melody, could be applied.

Dowland returns to recitative style to set the reiterations of the word 'pitty.' He divides the repetitions into two groups of three words and introduces musical *climax* to heighten the persuasive qualities of the textual *epizeuxis*. The carefully graduated increment of the rising *climax* not only increases the vehemence of the passion embodied in the word 'pitty' but also suggests a manner of delivery appropriate for this passage. The singer persuades the listener by degrees, as it were, and might underscore the first group with one of the postures for reinforcing the vehemence of a word (for example, plate 5 D) and utter the second group with greater intensity, emphasizing each reiteration of the sentiment by driving the extended right index down (plate 5 P). The reason Dowland dwells on 'pitty' becomes clear as the phrase continues. 'Pitty' is asked for help – now or never – and singers probably should draw attention to the antithetical nature of the text. The words 'now' and 'never' could be stressed, and the gesture for distinguishing contraries could be used to reinforce the voice; that is, the turned-up hand could be transferred from the left side of the body to the right (a suitable finger posture is given in plate 5 z).

'Pitty' is then implored to 'mark me not to endlesse paine,' and the expression of this sentiment is aided by textual *epizeuxis* coupled with musical *palillogia*. Here the freedom of the recitative-like style gives way to the slow tempo which parallels the sense of the words. For the repetition of 'mark me not to endlesse paine,' the separation of the second statement of the phrase from the first, so clearly indicated by Dowland in the vocal part, probably should be delayed slightly so that the articulation occurs after the ultimate note of the lutenist's phrase is played, that is, after the B♭ (the third crotchet of the bar). This reiteration, delivered with increased vehemence in the voice and reinforced by a forceful indicatory action in which the extended index finger admonishes pity not to inflict endless pain (plate 5 м), prepares the listener for the exclamatory 'alas I am condempne'd.' 'Alas' is, of course, one of the expletives which convey emotional outburst and should be emphasized with the voice and the hand. The singer might raise the hand aloft for the expletive (plate 3 o) and direct the hand toward himself for the remainder of the phrase (plate 3 ʟ). Once again, Dowland combines textual *epizeuxis* with musical *palillogia*, and these devices, together with the style of delivery they suggest, lead listeners to the climax of the phrase 'I am condempned ever.' The singer's increasing agitation, so carefully constructed by Dowland in an incremental way, can be made even more vehement if the speed of delivery, that is, the tempo, is accelerated for 'I am condempned ever.' A passionate application of the hand to the head (plate 2 ʟ) will help these words inflame the minds of listeners. Dowland ends the musical phrase with a cadence on the fifth above the final of the mode, the musical equivalent of a colon, and a pause at this point (by the singer and lutenist) allows the accumulated energy to dissipate, leaving listeners to anticipate what follows.

Dowland returns to recitative style, introduced through the lutenist's G-minor chord in the middle of bar 20, for the faltering realization that 'no hope' and 'no help' remain. Ascending musical *climax* accompanies these words and ensures that both singer and listener understand their implication: not only is there no hope but also there is no help for this 'woefull wretched wight,' and perhaps the words 'no help' could be uttered with even more vehemence. In fact, the greater vehemence of 'no help' can be underscored with a gesture which instantly enforces a word or idea such as the one shown in plate 5 I. Moreover, ample space should be left between the utterances so that the increasing desperation of the singer, intensified through sighs or sobs, will be deeply impressed upon the souls of listeners. The closing words of this period might be delivered with the utmost dismay and should be followed by the long pause the musical cadence suggests, for listeners now have a very weighty matter upon which to reflect.

But, of course, the story is not yet complete. The singer still must disclose the consequences of being condemned without hope or help. The music Dowland composes for this purpose depicts the plight of his 'wretched wight' quite literally. The descending minim line perfectly captures the sense of 'But downe, down, down, down I fall,' and the minims are delivered most affectively when a crescendo and decrescendo is performed on each one, the articulations required by the commas (*articulus*) helping the singer draw attention to each step of the steady descent. Listeners feel the passion of each repetition of 'downe' even more strongly, however, if the voice is enforced by an urging and pressing gesture (plate 5 D). Dowland further reinforces the pathos of the situation through musical *palillogia*, but the singer's suffering soon turns to hope as he begins to rise out of the depths of despair. This proves to be false hope, however, for it is crushed immediately with the words 'I never shall.' The rising vocal line, repeated by means of musical *synonymia*, is designed to reflect this feeling of hope, and its delivery is enhanced in two ways. First, the irony of this phrase will be heightened by the gesture for triumph (plate I P), and second, the notion of hope will be reinforced if the singer gradually increases the speed of delivery (tempo) during the second statement of 'downe and arise.' The excitement and anticipation generated by this latter effect should be carried forward by the lutenist, who would continue to accelerate the tempo (while the singer holds the long D) until the musical phrase is brought to a close on the second full crotchet of bar 25. At this point, the singer may wish to refer his hand to himself, using the time taken up by this action to allow the accumulated energy of the preceding phrase to subside before delivering 'I never shall,' the words which portray the bleak reality of the situation.

Dowland reinforces the passions embodied in this remarkable conclusion to the poem by repeating the entire period, thus creating in the song a tripartite structure of more or less equal proportions. The repetition of the final period may be delivered in a similar fashion, except that because Dowland has doubled the length of the singer's D on the reiteration of 'arise,' the acceleration of the tempo by the lutenist takes place over a longer musical phrase, and this makes it appropriate for the lutenist to introduce a ritardando just before the singer utters the final 'I never shall.' The only melodic embellishments I would suggest for the last two large sections of the piece are discrete cadential figures on 'doth remaine' and 'never shall.'

'In Darknesse Let Mee Dwell'

The poem 'In darknesse let mee dwell,' like 'Sorrow sorrow stay,' is infused with images of sorrow and grief (see pp 131–2). The striking *propositio* immediately invokes a sense of foreboding, and the words which follow depict a person so consumed with woe that his very existence seems to be a living death. Not only does the ground become sorrow but the roof of despair bars all light, the walls weep, and perhaps worst of all music has become a hellish cacophony. His fate is sealed, however, and he is resigned to living in darkness until death. These grave sentiments are intensified with numerous figures of repetition, and as in 'Sorrow sorrow stay,' these figures serve to transport the poem from the world of the written word to the realm of musical oration.

Ex 3.2 John Dowland, 'In darknesse let mee dwell' (1610 no 10)

Ex 3.2 *(continued)*

Dowland once again chooses the transposed *protus* mode for setting a text dealing with grief, but for this song the hypodorian mode is transposed to A (the so-called A-minor mode) rather than G (see Ex 3.2). He divides the song into two large sections and clearly marks the two parts by means of a double bar line. These sections encompass a number of commas, the very first one being for the lute alone. The lutenist's preamble, as it might be called, captures the character of the song right from the outset, for the opening musical gesture, an A-minor chord, serves to equate a doleful harmony with a woeful subject. Proceeding from this musical gesture, the lutenist establishes a tempo which reflects the grave subject matter of the poem (perhaps a crotchet = ca 92). At the close of this preamble, the singer's initial note emerges, almost imperceptibly at first, from the A-minor chord upon which the lutenist cadences. Dowland uses the singer's opening statement to frame the song, thus creating the musical counterpart of rhetorical *epanalepsis*.[6]

In order to intensify the image of grief, the singer might shake his head while contracting his eyebrows into a frown. At the word 'mee,' he should direct his hand toward himself. Care should be taken to observe the abrupt termination, the musical counterpart of *aposiopesis*, which closes the phrase. Dowland deliberately writes a remarkably short resolution to the *syncope*, and the duration of this note should be no longer than the crotchet he specifies. If he had wanted a longer note, he easily could have notated a minim instead of a crotchet followed by a rest. This hasty abandonment may well be meant to convey to listeners that even at the beginning of the song the singer's sorrow is almost too great for him to continue. In fact, the torment of the singer can be demonstrated most vehemently if the last note is uttered as a sob. Dowland separates the singer's opening phrase from the next one with a minim rest in both the voice and lute parts, and this leaves listeners ample time to consider the *propositio*.

The following textual phrases explain why the singer wishes to dwell in darkness, and his increasing despair gradually emerges as the poem unfolds. For 'The ground, the ground shall sorrow, sorrow be,' in addition to pronouncing the punctuation, each of the two uses of *epizeuxis* should be emphasized, and the underlying sentiment might be demon-

strated through the gesture for sorrow (plate 3 Y). This phrase, like the
previous one, seems to stand alone, and it might be brought to a close
with a slower speed of delivery, that is, a slowing of the tempo through a
ritardando, for the words 'sorrow be.' The next section ('The roofe
Dispaire to barre all, all cheerfull light from mee') begins afresh, as it
were, with a new melodic figure in the accompaniment. Here, the grow-
ing despair of the singer's situation might be demonstrated by lowering
the hands to the position for showing mental anguish (plate 1 K). The
anadiplosis in the middle of this phrase, that is, the reiteration of 'all,' is
separated by a rest in the vocal line, and this enables the singer to emphasize the repetition with a sigh as well as with increased intensity or volume. By the time the singer utters 'The wals of marble blacke that
moistned, that moistned still shall weepe, still shall weepe,' the third
statement to amplify the passion of despair, grief almost certainly is well
settled in the 'yearning bowels,' and this can be demonstrated most vehemently by touching the ends of the fingers to the breast. The crotchet
rest in the vocal line, which breaks up the words 'that moistned still shall
weepe,' undoubtedly represents a sob, and the comma at the end of this
phrase allows the singer time to sigh (using that sharp intake of breath
characteristic of Elizabethan sighing) at the high point of the phrase
(both musically and emotionally) before reinforcing the passionate appeal
of the words by repeating 'still shall weepe.'

The final and most damning depiction of the singer's grief is captured
in the words 'My musicke, My musicke hellish, hellish jarring sounds, jarring, jarring sounds to banish, banish friendly sleepe.' The *epizeuxis*
employed at the beginning of this phrase should be uttered with a most
anguished tonal quality in the voice, as this would serve to heighten the
realization that even music has become tormented. The singer is, of
course, speaking of himself at this point, and I suggest that the hand be
directed inward. But for the words 'hellish, hellish jarring sounds, jarring,
jarring sounds' one of the postures for urging and enforcing the sense of
the words might be adopted (for example, plate 5 D). At the words 'to
banish, banish friendly sleepe,' however, the singer might use the left
hand to repel the idea of sleep being banished (plate 3 M). Moreover, the
speed of delivery might quicken somewhat for the hellish jarring sounds,

and the lutenist should take care to emphasize the descending chromatic line which symbolizes the singer's plight. In general, the tonal quality of the voice in this passage should be harsh, reflecting the nature of the words. But the tone might very well soften somewhat when 'friendly sleepe' is uttered, and discrete ornamentation could be added just before the cadence note. These final words of the period draw the first part of the song to a close with a cadence on the fifth above the final, and listeners are led to expect much more to be spoken on the subject.

The second part opens with an A-major chord, and this sudden shift of *concentus* away from the minorish character of the mode may lead listeners to anticipate brighter sentiments. But this turns out to be a false expectation, for Dowland keeps listeners firmly anchored, both in text and music, to the passion of grief. However, the second part does seem to require a slightly faster speed of delivery, and a fairly lengthy pause between the two parts of the song enables listeners to reflect on the previous statements before new ideas are introduced. Right from the outset, completely overcome with grief, the singer resigns his liberty, becoming wedded to his woes and bedded to his tomb. The hands held forth together (plate 1 N) naturally express this state of mind and powerfully enforce the passionate appeal of the words. In fact, the word 'woes' might be selected for particular emphasis through a quick crescendo and decrescendo. This submission to sorrow leads the singer to explode in grief with the exclamation 'O Let me living die,' and Dowland's setting of these words may have been influenced by one of Giulio Caccini's songs (see Ex 3.3).

Ex 3.3 (a) Dowland 1610, 'In darknesse let mee dwell'
(b) Caccini 1601, 'Cor mio, deh non languire'

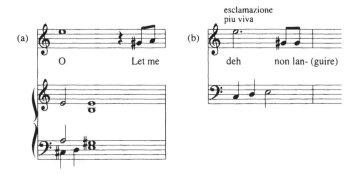

Hence, an *esclamazione*, coupled with the explosive gesture of clapping the left palm with the right fist (plate 1 G), seems most appropriate for intensifying this sudden outburst. Dowland repeats the words through musical *climax* and extends the entire phrase by means of *epizeuxis*. For the second exclamation, add an under-third elevation, while raising the hand aloft, and use the punctuation which separates the repeated words and phrases to draw attention to the increasing emphasis being placed on the word 'living.'

The textual idea which began in the exclamation is not completed, however, until the singer utters 'Till death, till death doe come.' The *epizeuxis* in this phrase needs to be emphasized by the singer, and Dowland further draws attention to the sentiment expressed in the phrase by repeating it twice, the first time using musical *palillogia* to underscore the text and the second time using a melody which lends itself to further intensification during its delivery. Each iteration, separated by commas, should be more anguished than the previous one, and the third statement might be reinforced through a crescendo on the dotted semibreve which is articulated at its highest point just before the *epizeuxis*. Moreover, the incremental progression of intensification that Dowland's melodic design suggests can be enhanced in a most striking way if hand gestures are organized in a similarly progressive manner. For the first iteration, one might assume a posture of extreme loathing (plate 3 w), placing the hands a short distance from the chest. On the second statement, the hands could be pushed out a little further, but on the third iteration, the utmost detestation can be shown by driving the hands out to the left side while turning the head to the right (plate 3 v).

However, in order to surprise and delight listeners with the *epanalepsis* which closes the song, the performers might wish to give the impression that the song ends at the lutenist's cadence at the beginning of the second last bar. This effect may be achieved most persuasively if the final utterance of 'till death doe come' is delivered as if it actually were the last statement of the song, the lutenist seeming to bring the piece to a close on the final of the mode at the beginning of the second last bar. But Dowland toys with the listeners' expectations here, for although the performers certainly can approach this cadence as though it were the final one, Dowland carefully avoids the cadence by leaping from G♯ to C. At this point, listeners are unsure of what to expect next, and a pause after the lutenist's cadence serves to heighten their anticipation, the ensuing *epanalepsis* truly delighting their ears while stirring their minds. Undoubtedly, the repetition of 'In darknesse let mee dwell' reminds listeners of the *propositio* and leaves them with a weighty matter to ponder. In fact, it is only at the end of the song that the full force of the abrupt termination Dowland has composed is impressed on listeners and that Dowland's reason for incorporating the musical counterpart of *aposiopesis* becomes clear. This figure enables the singer to penetrate deeply into the souls of listeners with a powerful demonstration of the depth to which grief has settled, his sorrow being so great at this point that he really cannot continue even though the musical cadence (on the fifth above the final of the mode) which underpins this device leads listeners to expect much more to be spoken on the subject. The effect of the abrupt termination can be enhanced most vehemently if the singer, at the same time he utters the last note of the song with a sob, simultaneously drives the hands out to either side in a violent motion designed to double the passion of abhorrence.

Passionate ayres represent some of the loftiest and most affective musical orations of the early seventeenth century. These ayres are full of auricular and sententious devices which give songs efficacy, that is, the power to move listeners. With figures, singers persuade both copiously and vehemently, sung discourse achieving its greatest persuasivenes and hence its highest style when it is adorned with figures which at once both delight the ear and stir the mind. Audiences from the early seventeenth century similarly disciplined in the art of rhetoric would have appreciated these matters and taken pleasure from a presentation which, through the combination of intellectual prowess and vehement delivery, was designed so that it 'moveth affections wonderfully' (Peacham the Elder 1577 f P3v). Moreover, Dowland's skilful handling of the techniques of *elocutio* to effect an imitation of man's actions and passions demonstrates his mastery of affective persuasion. Today, a knowledge of the rhetorical basis of the passionate ayre enables modern performers to recreate the early seventeenth-century style of eloquent delivery from within known tenets of the time. By recovering the principles with which English singers of the period probably were thoroughly familiar, we are able to bridge the gap which exists between historical documents, the artefacts of their culture, and actual modern performance. We now can begin to develop an intuitive understanding of their music and of approaches to its performance.

# NOTES

Introduction

1 Collingwood 1961 (p 155). For further discussion of Collingwood's work
   and for a more fully developed statement on how contextual discussions
   of cultural history relate to musicology, see Tomlinson 1984, 1988.
2 Johannes Nucius in his *Musices poeticae* (Neisse 1613 f A4r) names
   Dunstaple as one of the first rhetorically expressive composers, and the
   rhetorical implications of two works by Dufay are discussed in Elders
   1981. The rhetorical connotations of the term *imitatio* in the late
   fifteenth and sixteenth centuries are discussed in Brown 1982. The
   rhetorical basis of poetry, painting, and music in Italy and France
   between 1550 and 1650 is treated in LeCoat 1975.
3 The importance of the passions to Renaissance rhetoricians has been
   summarized in Vickers 1982.
4 I will make regular reference to Quintilian throughout the book, for
   although he is a classical author, Quintilian was an important source for
   Elizabethan and Jacobean rhetoricians. On the influence of Quintilian in
   the late sixteenth and early seventeenth centuries, see Colson 1924
   (pp lxiv–lxxxix), Howell 1961 (passim), and Sonnino 1968 (p 2).
5 Thomas Elyot defined eloquence in relation to speaking: 'Undoubtedly
   very eloquence is in every tonge where any matter or act done or to be
   done is expressed in wordes, cleane, propise, ornate, and comely, wherof

sentences be so aptly compact, that they by a vertue inexplicable, do draw unto them the mindes and consent of the hearers, beynge therewith either persuaded, meved, or to delectacion induced' (1546 f 40v).

6 The most thorough study of English grammar-school education of this period is still Baldwin 1944. Vickers (1988 pp 255–70) provides an excellent summary not only of the methods of teaching rhetoric but also of the importance of rhetoric in Elizabethan and Jacobean society.

7 However, I fall short of truly achieving the thickest context, for many facets of the culture of the period that impinge on music fall beyond the scope of this book.

8 Speaking and singing appear to have remained closely connected in England until at least the middle of the nineteenth century. Several writers from the eighteenth and nineteenth centuries declare that singing should be based directly on speaking and that singers should use the orator as a model. In the eighteenth century, Anselm Bayly writes in his *A Practical Treatise on Singing and Playing with Just Expression and Real Elegance* (London 1771): 'Recitative is an expressive and elegant manner of speaking ... let them [singers] ask themselves how an orator would pronounce them [the words in recitatives], preserving the grammatical connection, touching lightly, without any appoggiatura, short syllables and unimportant words, and giving a due, but not fierce, energy to the emphatic' (p 60). In the nineteenth century, Richard Bacon, Isaac Nathan, and Manuel Garcia give similar instructions. Bacon, in *Elements of Vocal Science* (London 1824; ed Edward Foreman [Champaign, Ill, 1966]), states: 'The effects of reading or declamation are produced by the quality of tone, by inflexion, by emphasis, and by total cessations or pauses. Singing seems only to heighten these effects by using in a bolder manner the same agents. The principles of both are the same ... The student [of singing] ought first to consider the appropriate delivery of the words before he tries them in combination with the air. Having thus determined how the words ought to be read [spoken aloud], he will proceed in the adaptation of them to melody' (pp 73, 78). Nathan asserts: 'We may account oratory, the twin-sister of music:– in both, expression holds the same inalienable sway ... In oratory the requisition of accurate pronunciation, management of the voice, and appropriate gesture were particulars, which completely identified this subject [oratory] with that now under discussion [singing]. Hence, considering oratory as a science congener to music, as far as *expression* goes, we shall apply the one to the other' (*Musurgia Vocalis* [London 1836] pp 223–4). And Garcia maintains:

'A pupil [of singing], in order to discover the tone [of voice] suitable to each sentiment, should attentively study the words of his part, make himself acquainted with every particular relating to the personage that he is to represent, and recite [that is, speak] his *rôle* as naturally as if giving utterance to his own feelings' (*Garcia's New Treatise on the Art of Singing* [London 1857] p 67; I am quoting from the edition published in Boston during the 1870s).

9 See Poulton 1982 (chap 1 passim) for a discussion of the literary tributes made to Dowland.

10 Mellers 1965, Pattison 1970, Smith 1973, Spink 1974, Jorgens 1982, Poulton 1982, Rooley 1983, Toft 1984, and Wells 1984, 1985. See Toft 1984 and Wells 1984, 1985 for discussions of music and rhetoric in the works of John Dowland.

Chapter 1   *Elocutio*

1 Some rhetoricians, for example Puttenham (1589 pp 245–6) and Peacham the Elder (1577 ff 02r–03v), distinguish between *prosopopoeia* (making senseless, dumb, or inanimate things speak) and *prosopographia* (feigning the nature of absent persons), but Peacham the Younger seems to have known the definition I have quoted from Fraunce.

2 Wilson (1553 pp 338–9) defines the term exornation as 'a gorgiousse beautifiynge of the tongue with borowed wordes, and chaung of sentence or speache, with muche varietie.'

3 Curiously, despite what we know about English education of the period (see especially Baldwin 1944 and the summaries in Sister Joseph 1947 [pp 8–13], Vickers 1988 [pp 255–70], and Vickers 1989 [pp 45–53]), one recent writer, Elise Jorgens, maintains that a reader of the time 'certainly was not expected to analyze [in poems] the conventions of rhetoric' (1982 p 222). Her statement obviously contravenes the remarks by Peacham quoted here.

4 For a discussion of the various ways in which the terms trope and scheme were defined historically, see Lanham 1968 (pp 101–3).

5 Wells (1985 pp 520ff) discusses the importance of the complaint for English song-writers of the early seventeenth century.

6 Cited in Sister Joseph 1947 (pp 87–9).

7 See, for example, Campion, Coprario, Dowland, Ford, Jones, Morley, Pilkington, and Rosseter.

8 The unadorned poem is found in Coprario 1606 (no 4).

9 For similar examples from the works of Shakespeare, see Sister Joseph 1947 (pp 82–3).

10 Dowland appears to have supplied two separate poems for the song, one with two verses and the other with four. All of the editions of *The First Booke of Songes or Ayres* (1597, 1600, 1603, 1606, and 1613) number the verses 1, 2 and 1, 2, 3, 4 (note, however, that the Giles Earle Songbook [British Library, ms Add 24665, p 22] numbers the verses from 1 to 6). The two poems are complete within themselves and express distinct but related sentiments. In the first poem (given above), the speaker literally dies in the second verse. It makes little sense, therefore, for the poem to continue. The other poem, however, presents a new story, the first two verses being contrasted: 'All the day' versus 'All the night.' Structurally, the last two lines of each verse in this second poem are quite different from the equivalent lines in the first poem. *Auxesis* is not present in the penultimate lines, and the ultimate lines contain eight syllables rather than ten. Dowland's reason for including two poems remains obscure unless, of course, he simply wanted to supply a longer, alternate poem for those who wished more verses to sing. The second poem is given below.

>All the day the sun that lends me shine,
>By frownes doth cause me pine,
>And feeds mee with delay:
>Her smiles, my springs, that makes my joyes to grow,
>Her frownes the winters of my woe:
>
>All the night my sleepes are full of dreames,
>My eyes are full of streames.
>My heart takes no delight,
>To see the fruits and joyes that some do find,
>And marke the stormes are mee assignde.
>
>Out alas, my faith is ever true,
>Yet will she never rue,
>Nor yeeld me any grace:
>Her eyes of fire, her heart of flint is made,
>Whom teares, nor truth may once invade.

Gentle love draw forth thy wounding dart,
Thou canst not peerce her heart.
For I that doe approve,
By sighs and teares more hot then are thy shafts,
Did tempt while she for triumph laughs.

11 See Wells 1984 (pp 181–2) for a discussion of the other figures present
in this verse of the poem.

12 Various *musica poetica* theorists assign rhetorical terms to somewhat
divergent musical procedures, and no standardized definitions of either
rhetorical or rhetorical/musical figures appear to have existed in the
sixteenth and seventeenth centuries. On the surface, then, some of the
connections between rhetorical and musical definitions can seem tenuous
(see Vickers 1984 for a discussion of what he considers, too harshly in my
view, as several problems). But if one searches carefully, useful rhetorical
parallels do emerge, and in those cases where close connections exist,
the rhetorical background of the musical procedure often helps to clarify
the intent of the musical device. I will cite, therefore, those musical and
rhetorical definitions which seem to be the most closely related. Unfortunately, we do not know which rhetorical definitions music theorists
might have known, and this forces me to supply a suitable rhetorical
definition without being able to prove that the music theorist in question
actually knew that definition. Moreover, I derive some of the definitions
of musical figures from treatises written in other countries. Nevertheless,
my study proceeds on an empirical basis, for even though a fairly large
number of musical-rhetorical devices were defined in late sixteenth- and
early seventeenth-century English treatises (nineteen are listed in Butler
1980), the definitions of some of the figures present in English lute-songs
are to be found only in foreign treatises. The authors of some of these
treatises, such as Joachim Burmeister and Johannes Nucius, were contemporary with the lute-song repertoire, whereas others, such as
Christoph Bernhard, were not.

13 Walther (1708 ii 6, p 158) mentions *synonymia* but does not define it,
referring the reader to Johann G. Ahle's *Musikalisches Sommer-Gespräche*
(1697) for elaboration. Ahle, however, gives only a rhetorical definition
of the term (see Bartel 1985 pp 269–70), but the musical equivalent is
encountered frequently in the early seventeenth-century lute-song repertoire. Therefore, in following the practices of early seventeenth-century
theorists, I apply the rhetorical term to an analogous compositional tech-

nique, bringing my use of the term into line with that established in Buelow 1980.

14 For an account of the earlier versions of this poem, which were sung for Elizabeth I, see Doughtie 1970 (pp 540–1).

15 I will adapt early seventeenth-century definitions of the term to suit the song repertoire, using *climax* for single repetitions of a melodic fragment and *gradatio* for extensions of the figure beyond one restatement.

16 Similar descriptions are given in Wilson 1553 (p 396) and Peacham the Elder 1577 (f M2v).

17 For woe, see Dowland 1612 (nos 10, 15); for bitter grief, see Campion 1613/2 (no 21); for sorrow, see Ford 1607 (no 5; Ex 1.17 below); for mists and darkness, see Campion 1613/1 (no 1); and for tears, see Dowland 1597 (no 14).

18 See also the collection of examples in Sonnino 1968 (p 88).

19 Specific suggestions for delivering this figure, based on techniques for varying dynamics on single notes, will be given in *'Passionate Ayres Pronounced.'*

20 For depictions of rising, see Danyel 1606 (no 19), Jones 1600 (no 9), and Jones 1601 (nos 1, 18, 21). For representations of falling, see Danyel 1606 (no 10), Dowland 1600 (nos 2, 3), Dowland 1612 (no 19), and Jones 1600 (no 21). For depictions of sighs, see Dowland 1612 (no 10), Jones 1605 (no 7), and Jones 1609 (no 17). The relish is imitated in Danyel 1606 (no 4).

21 The extension of a dissonance beyond the normal expectation is called *prolongatio* (Bartel 1985 pp 243–4).

22 For another example of the inappropriateness of the music for later verses of strophic songs, see the discussion of Dowland's 'His golden locks' (1597 no 18) in *'Pronunciatio'* ('All the senses satisfied'). With so many songs suffering from the same problem, I am puzzled by the latter portion of Elise Jorgens' statement regarding Elizabethan strophic song: 'The stanzas of the Elizabethan song poem often were parallel statements, with little or no narrative continuity from one stanza to the next and without appreciable change in tone, so that the same musical interpretation would be appropriate for all stanzas and musical structure would reinforce poetic structure' (Jorgens 1982 p 15). However, part of her statement on later metaphysical poetry seems equally applicable to the 'Elizabethan song poem': 'to sing succeeding stanzas to the same music as the first is in a sense a contradiction of the poetic structure' (p 15).

23 On the various ascriptions for this poem, see Doughtie 1970 (pp 520–1).
24 See also Dowland's setting of the first and third lines of 'Weepe you no more sad fountaines' (1603 no 15).
25 Peacham the Elder asserts that with *propositio (prolepsis)* we state in a 'few wordes the summe of that matter, whereof we presently intend to speake' (1577 f s2v).

Chapter 2   *Pronunciatio*

1 Adapted from Wright 1604 (p 172)
2 Michel Le Faucheur's treatise *Traitte de l'action de l'orateur ou de la Prononciation et du geste* (Paris 1657), translated into English as *An Essay upon the Action of an Orator, as to his Pronunciation and Gesture* (London, undated), is a most useful source for a documenting of seventeenth-century techniques of delivery. Although a French source, his discussion parallels that found in English treatises, both Le Faucheur and his English counterparts basing their work on classical authors. The value of Le Faucheur's treatise for my study lies in its detailed description of the techniques for varying the voice according to figures and passions, a subject dealt with by English writers in a much less developed fashion. I will quote from Le Faucheur when it is necessary to flesh out techniques to which English authors allude without fully explaining the desired effect. The English translation, thought to date from around either 1680 or 1700, demonstrates that Le Faucheur's treatment of the subject circulated in England from at least that time.
3 Brinsley 1612 (pp 213–14)
4 On speaking from memory, see Quintilian (xi pp 256–7) and Mulcaster 1581 (p 57); and on deriving the style of delivery from the affections in a text, see Fraunce 1588 (ii chap 2) and Wright 1604 (pp 132, 178–83).
5 An important aspect of historical delivery, namely regional accents in spoken English, will not be discussed here. I refer readers to the work of Eric J. Dobson (1968) for a lengthy discussion of this aspect of pronunciation.
6 Granger (1616 f o3v) uses the term punctuation, but the words distinctions and points seem to have been more common.
7 Wright 1604 (p 179)
8 The list and succeeding definitions were derived from Hart 1551 and

1569, Lily 1567, Mulcaster 1582, Clement 1587, Granger 1616, Butler 1633, Robinson 1641 (based on Lily 1567), and Smith 1657.

9   That the phrase 'tone of voice' includes both pitch and volume is made clear in Charles Butler's discussion of *ecphonesis*. See below for the relevant quotation.

10 Perfect primary cadences are formed on the final of the mode and come to rest on an octave or unison (1636 pp 66, 82). Butler considers perfect cadences to be secondary when they are formed on the fifth, third, or fourth (in order of importance) step of the scale (1636 p 83). Imperfect cadences signify that the harmony or ditti will rest very little, for both music and words are to proceed further. In these cadences, either the voice rising to the cadence note drops out or it forms a third, fifth, or sixth with the bass (1636 p 67). Presumably, imperfect cadences also could be primary or secondary in function. Improper cadences, on the other hand, are formed on the sixth, second, or seventh step of the scale and are used sparingly, as they are 'strange and informal to the Air' (1636 p 83).

11 The discussion of musical cadences in grammatical terms is, of course, much older than Zarlino, Morley, and Butler. Medieval treatises establish the connection (see Crane 1960 pp 29–78), and Zarlino probably knew the writings of Giovanni del Lago (1540 pp 39ff). The following is a summary of Zarlino's discussion.

12 Moreover, Fellowes' editions (revised by Dart) of Dowland's songs are much more faithful to the punctuation of the original than is one of the most recent editions of lute-songs (see Greer, who states that 'spelling, punctuation and capitalization have been modernized' [1987 p xxii]). It strikes me as odd that an editor quite arbitrarily would choose to modernize certain aspects of early seventeenth-century songs but not others. What results is a most unsatisfactory mix of the old and the new.

13 Modern singers sometimes apply musical solutions to what are essentially dramatic problems. In certain strophic songs which lend themselves to melodic embellishment, some singers prefer to delight listeners with *auricular* pleasures alone, adding more and more divisions as the verses progress, instead of concentrating on projecting the story to the listeners (the *sententious* approach to interpretation). See, for example, the recordings of Dowland's 'Now O now' (1597 no 6) by Ian Partridge (*It Fell on a Summer's Day, Songs by Dowland and Campion*, Hyperion Records) and Paul Hillier (*English Ayres and Duets*, Hyperion Records).

14 On Diana Poulton's conjectured existence of a 1608 edition, see Doughtie 1970 (p 66).

15   The rests I have inserted to parallel the punctuation of the text should
     not be interpreted too literally, either in duration or in placement.

16   Lines 4 and 5 of the third verse follow 1597, 1600, and 1603 in using
     'her' and 'Goddes' instead of 'him' and 'Yee gods' (note that 1603 has
     'Gods'). The song was first performed before Queen Elizabeth at the
     accession tilt of 17 November 1590 (see Doughtie 1970 p 466), but as
     Elizabeth died in 1603, subsequent editions were changed. I have
     restored this aspect of the poem to its original intention.

17   See the discussion of this figure in *'Elocutio.'*

18   Although Hobbes' treatise is a translation of Aristotle's *Rhetoric*, these
     remarks seem to have originated with Hobbes. See Hobbes 1637 (p 108,
     n 3 of the modern editor).

19   On the latter understanding, see Le Faucheur 1657 (p 130) where
     'Elevated Tone' means raised in volume; see also the expressions *'Tone'*
     and *'louder Voyce'* on p 128.

20   Le Faucheur labels this figure *anadiplosis*.

21   Le Faucheur labels this figure *epizeuxis*.

22   A translation of ff Ssiii–Ssivv of Bk v appears in MacClintock 1979
     (pp 62–5).

23   Three notable exceptions are the recording of Henry Purcell's *Dido and
     Aeneas* under the direction of Andrew Parrott, especially the characters of
     the Sorceress and the Enchantresses (Chandos Records), and Julianne
     Baird's recordings of Robert Johnson's 'Come away, Hecate' (*The English
     Lute Song*, Dorian Recordings) and Henry Purcell's 'Bess of Bedlam'
     (*English Mad Songs and Ayres*, Dorian Recordings).

24   The manuscripts to which I refer are:
     1   Cambridge, King's College, Rowe 2 (Francis Turpyn's songbook).
     ˙   Rastall (1973) dates the manuscript ca 1610–15 or even a little ear-
         lier. Oboussier (1953 p 149) dates it roughly 1610–15.
     2   London, British Library, Add 15117. Joiner (1969 pp 51ff) prefers a
         date after 1614, and Jorgens (1986–9 vol 1, p v) suggests ca 1614–16.
     3   Oxford, Bodleian Library, Tenbury 1018, 1019. Spink (1966 p 136)
         dates both ca 1615.
     4   Dublin, Trinity College, F.5.13. Spink (1986 p 272) suggests a date
         of ca 1615, and the arguments in Till (1975 p 52) indicate a date
         before 1618–20.
     5   London, British Library, Egerton 2971 (Robertus Downes' song-
         book). Dart (1961 p 31) proposes a date no earlier than 1610 and no
         later than 1622.

6 London, British Library, Add 24665 (Giles Earle's songbook).The manuscript carries the date 1615, and Till (1975 p 53) maintains that it was compiled between 1615 and 1626, with the bulk of the lute-songs being copied by 1620.

7 Oxford, Christ Church Library, 439. Jorgens (1986–9 vol 6, p v) dates the manuscript before 1620, with Till (1975 p 51) suggesting ca 1610 or later, but Spink (1966 p 133) proposes ca 1620–30.

8 Cambridge, Fitzwilliam Museum, Mu 782 (formerly 52.D.25). Till (1975 p 52) dates the songs in the manuscript between 1618 and the early 1620s, and Spink (1986 p 272) suggests ca 1620 or later. Fenlon (1982 p 149), on the other hand, believes the songs in question, that is, those on ff 98v–116r, were added ca 1650.

9 Oxford, Christ Church Library, 87 (Elizabeth Davenant's songbook). The manuscript carries the date 1624, and Spink (1966 p 134) points out that the songs up to f 19 were written in Davenant's time, for an acrostic on her name appears on f 19 after the last song. Cutts (1959 p 29) suggests that the songs were copied before 1624, but Jorgens (1986–9 vol 7, p v) believes that the copying began ca 1624 and continued for several years.

10 London, British Library, Add 29481. Spink (1986 p 272) states that it probably dates from before 1630, while Duckles (1957 p 343) lists it as one of the sources copied before 1625. Till (1975 p 79) dates the manuscript ca 1620, and Jones (1989 p 118) believes that ff 2–26v probably were copied in the 1620s.

25 Further discussion of the differences between graces and divisions is found in Poulton 1975 (p 107) and Jones 1989 (pp 52–4).

26 Philip Brett has edited the song in its consort setting (1967 pp 10–2) and has included divisions from Turpyn. Brett omits some of the divisions and changes the rhythm in one passage (Brett's bar 22).

27 For a more fully developed discussion of this style, see Brown 1973–4.

28 Earle owned the book when it was being compiled; therefore I presume that he was a singer.

29 Earle probably copied the volume himself. If the words 'Giles Earle his booke 1615' on f 3r are in Earle's own hand, then he must have copied the rest of the book as well, for most of the manuscript appears to be in the same hand.

30 Although not discussed here, see the setting of 'Drowne not with teares' on f 112v.

31 But in 'Have you seene the white lilly grow' (f 4v), rhythmic expansion occurs frequently.

32 I have included one grace from an early seventeenth-century source, that is, the relish as described in Robinson (T) 1603.

33 Heywood separates action from the other parts of *pronunciatio*.

34 Poulton 1980 (pp 211–12), corrected in Wilson 1991 (p 580). This preface may have been written by Thomas Campion, as the volume also contains his songs. Unfortunately, there is no reliable way of determining which man actually wrote the preface, and I simply presume that it was the work of Rosseter.

35 Bulwer concurs (1644 p 241).

36 See also Fraunce 1588 (f J4v).

37 Abraham Fraunce concurs, except that he advocates extending the middle finger (1588 f κ4r). Fraunce lists several other positions of the fingers (1588 ff κ3v–κ4r), and all of these differ from Bulwer's use of the same or similar positions. For example, Bulwer's drawing in plate 4 Q represents irony or mockery, whereas Fraunce describes it as an urgent and insistent gesture. Furthermore, the position shown in Bulwer's plate 4 O is an expression of scorn and contempt, but for Fraunce it is simply an indicatory gesture, pointing at or showing something.

38 This gesture also may be used to signify shame and admiration.

39 This gesture also depicts fear, abasement of mind, and abject and vanquished courage.

40 It also may be used to bid farewell.

41 This gesture also may signify duty and reverence.

42 In ancient times, Bulwer maintains, orators kept the right hand within their cloaks as an expression of modesty.

43 Also suitable for shame and great grief.

44 Bulwer also includes a lengthy section called 'The Apochrypha of Action' which lists those things that truly are outside rhetorical decorum (1644 pp 214–38).

Chapter 3   *Passionate Ayres Pronounced*

1 See the quote from Peacham cited in the 'Introduction.'

2 I have supplied the punctuation in square brackets to help articulate the sense of the sentences and to bring the textual pointing into line with Dowland's musical punctuation.

3 The possibility that Dowland himself may have reversed the order is sug-

gested in Poulton 1982 (p 319), though the rhetorical significance of this change is not commented upon there.

4   See Caccini's discussion of crescendo and decrescendo *(il crescere e sce-mare della voce)* and *esclamazione* in the preface to his *Le nuove musiche* (1601). Both 'Sorrow sorrow stay' and 'In darknesse let mee dwell' contain a number of passages that show Italian influence. This is particularly true of the recitative-like passages and one phrase in 'In darknesse let mee dwell' which may have been derived directly from Caccini (see Ex 3.3 below). Dowland had travelled to Italy, and it is not surprising to see Italian traits in his music. I will suggest, therefore, Italianate devices where appropriate.

5   See the preface to Caccini 1601 for a discussion of *esclamazioni.*

6   The relationship between rhetorical and musical figures in this passage is discussed in *'Elocutio'* in conjunction with Ex 1.20.

 GLOSSARY

affections	see passions
anabasis	an ascending melody used to depict the sense of the words (Bartel 1985 pp 84–5)
anadiplosis	a figure in which the last word of one clause becomes the first word of the next (Peacham the Elder 1577 f J3r)
anaphora	a figure in which the same word is iterated at the beginning of successive sentences (Fraunce 1588 chap 19)
anastrophe	a figure containing a preposterous ordering of words which runs contrary to normal speaking (Sherry 1550 p 31)
antithesis	a figure which 'is a proper coupling togeather of contraries, and it is eyther in wordes that be contrary, or in contrary sentences' (Peacham the Elder 1577 f R1r)
aposiopesis	a figure denoting abrupt terminations: 'when through some affection, as of feare, anger, sorrow, bashfulnesse, and such like, we breake of[f] our speech, before it be all ended' (Peacham the Elder 1577 f N1v)
articulus	a figure which separates 'words & clauses one from another, either by distinguishing the sound [with commas], or by separating the sense' (Peacham the Elder 1593 p 56)
auricular figures	those whose purpose simply was to delight the ear: 'not onely the whole body of a tale in a poeme or historie may be made in such sort pleasant and agreable to the

eare, but also every clause by it selfe, and every single word carried in a clause, may have their pleasant sweetenesse apart' (Puttenham 1589 pp 171–2)

auxesis a figure involving an ascent by degrees to the top of some matter as 'when we make our saying grow and increase by an orderly placing of our words, making the latter word always exceed the former, in force of signifyca-tion ... In this fygure, order must be dilligently observed, that the stronger may follow the weaker, and the worthyer the lesse worthy' (Peacham the Elder 1577 f Q2v).

cadences resting points in music equivalent to punctuation in language; types (all from Butler 1636):

1) perfect – the voices come to rest on an octave or unison; perfect cadences are primary if they are formed on the final of the mode and secondary if formed on the fifth, third, or fourth (in order of importance) step of the scale (pp 66, 82–3)

2) imperfect – the voice rising to the cadence note drops out or it forms a third, fifth, or sixth with the bass; presum-ably imperfect cadences could be primary or secondary in function (p 67)

3) improper – the voices come to rest on the sixth, second, or seventh step of the scale, and because these cadences are 'strange and informal to the Air,' they are used sparingly (p 83)

catabasis a descending melody used to depict the sense of the words (Bartel 1985 pp 115–16)

clausula cadence

climax (gradatio) rhetoric: a figure in which 'the worde, whiche endeth the sentence goyng before, doeth begin the nexte' (Wilson 1553 pp 405–6)

music: the stepwise repetition of a melodic fragment (Bartel 1985 pp 122–7); I adapt early seventeenth-century defi-nitions of the term to suit the song repertoire, using *climax* for single repetitions and *gradatio* for extensions of the figure beyond one restatement.

colon the punctuation mark ':' or the segment of a sentence preced-ing the colon (it often consists of one or more commas)

comma	the punctuation mark ',' or the segment of a sentence preceding the comma
concentus	the vertical combination of notes sounding together
dialogism	a figure 'where *two Persons* are brought in as 'twere *Dialoguing* one another, one of 'em moving the *Question* and t'other making the *Answer*, you must change your *voyce* by turns, as if *two Men* were really a talking together' (Le Faucheur 1657 p 135)
distinctions	punctuation (comma, semicolon, colon, period, question mark, exclamation mark, round brackets)
ditti	the words of a song
divisions	figural patterns which embellish several or many notes by dividing longer notes into shorter ones
ecphonesis	a figure 'when through affection either of anger, sorrow, gladnesse, marveyling, feare, or any such lyke, we breake out in voyce with an exclamation, & outcry to expresse the passions of our minde, after this manner. O lamentable estate, O cursed misery, O wicked impudency, O joy imcomparable, O rare and singuler bewty' (Peacham the Elder 1577 f κ4r)
eloquence	'where any matter or act done or to be done is expressed in wordes, cleane, propise, ornate, and comely, wherof sentences be so aptly compact, that they by a vertue inexplicable, do draw unto them the mindes and consent of the hearers, beynge therewith either persuaded, meved, or to delectacion induced' (Elyot 1546 f 40v)
emphasis	a figure whose purpose is to 'inforce the sence of any thing by a word of more than ordinary efficacie' (Puttenham 1589 p 194)
enargia	Puttenham's class of figures whose purpose was to 'satisfie and delight th'eare onely by a goodly outward shew set upon the matter with wordes, and speaches smothly and tunably running' (1589 p 155)
energia	Puttenham's class of figures that worked inwardly to stir the mind 'by certaine intendments or sence of such wordes and speaches' (1589 p 155)
epanalepsis	a figure in which a sentence begins and ends with the same word (Peacham the Elder 1593 p 46)
epimone	a figure involving the regular repetition of one phrase at

	equal distance because that phrase 'beareth the whole burden of the song' (Puttenham 1589 p 233)
epistrophe	a figure in which the same word is iterated at the end of successive sentences (Hoskins 1599 p 127)
epizeuxis	a figure involving the immediate restatement of a word or two for greater vehemency (Peacham the Elder 1577 f J3r)
esclamazione	a certain strengthening of the relaxed voice, for example, a quick decrescendo followed by a rapid crescendo (Caccini 1601 preface)
figure	a form of speech artfully varied from common usage (Quintilian IX pp 352–5), or 'a certaine lively or good grace set upon wordes, speaches and sentences to some purpose and not in vaine, giving them ornament or efficacie by many manner of alterations in shape, in sounde, and also in sence, sometime by way of surplusage, sometime by defect, sometime by disorder, or mutation, and also by putting into our speaches more pithe and substance, subtilitie, quicknesse, efficacie or moderation, in this or that sort tuning and tempring them, by amplification, abridgement, opening, closing, enforcing, meekening or otherwise disposing them to the best purpose' (Puttenham 1589 p 171)
fuga	point of imitation
graces	small melodic figures, frequently of no more than a few notes, which embellish single notes
gradatio	see *climax* (music)
heterolepsis	a leap from a consonant note to a dissonant one (Bartel 1985 pp 184–6)
hypotyposis	rhetoric: a large group of figures which are directed toward lively description or counterfeit representation (Puttenham 1589 p 245)
	music: a generic term for any musical device that serves to illustrate the text in a literal fashion (Bartel 1985 pp 196–8)
hypozeuxis	a figure in which the language is adorned by supplying the same word in more than one clause (Puttenham 1589 pp 177–8)
member	the segment of a sentence enclosed by two punctuation marks

mutatio toni	an abrupt change in *concentus* for expressive purposes (Bartel 1985 pp 216–19)
palillogia	rhetoric: a figure which serves to add weight to the idea expressed in the text by emphasizing a particular aspect of its meaning, as 'when the word repeated hath another signification' (Peacham the Elder 1577 f J2v [Diaphora])
	music: a figure involving the repetition of a melodic fragment at the same pitch (Bartel 1985 pp 222–4)
paronomasia	a figure in which 'a word is changed in signification by changing of a letter or sillable' (Fraunce 1588 chap 24)
parrhesia	rhetoric: the use of pungent language to reprehend the hearers for some fault (*Rhetorica* IV pp 348–55)
	music: the *mi–fa* clash of the false relation or other dissonances between parts (Bartel 1985 pp 231–3)
passions	'none other thyng, but a stirryng, or forcyng of the mynde, either to desier, or elles to detest, and lothe any thyng, more vehemently then by nature we are commonly wonte to doe' (Wilson 1553 p 266); passions are caused by certain internal acts or operations of the soul which stir in the mind and alter the humours of the body; they are things such as love, pain, ire, joy, fear, hope, flight, hatred, etc (Wright 1604 pp 8, 33–4)
pathopoeia	rhetoric: the generic term for two categories of rhetorical devices that move the minds of listeners to indignation, anger, fear, envy, hatred, hope, gladness, mirth, laughter, sorrow, or sadness; the first type is called imagination and embraces 'sharp figures' that stir the sorts of vehement affections that one finds in tragedy, that is, matters which are great, cruel, horrible, marvellous, pleasant, etc; the second type is called commiseration through which the orator brings his listeners to tears or moves them to pity or forgiveness (Sherry 1550 p 68, Peacham the Elder 1577 f P3r).
	music: chromaticism (Bartel 1985 pp 234–6)
period	the punctuation mark '.' or the accumulated segments of a sentence preceding the period
point	'a certain number and order of observable Notes in any one Parte, iterated in the same or in divers Partes' (Butler 1636 p 71)

prolongatio	the extension of a dissonance beyond the normal expectation (Bartel 1985 p 243)
propositio	when orators state in a 'few wordes the summe of that matter, whereof we presently intend to speake' (Peacham the Elder 1577 f s2v)
prosopopoeia	'a fayning of any person, when in our speach we represent the person of anie, and make it [him] speake as though he were there present' (Fraunce 1588 f G2r); the orator personifies the inner thoughts and affections of an absent person, making that person actually seem to appear before the eyes of the hearer (Quintilian IX pp 390–1, Peacham the Elder 1577 f O2r–v).
rhetoric	'the science, wherby is taughte an artificiall fourme of spekyng, wherin is the power to perswade, move, and delyte' (Elyot 1546 f 41v); traditionally, the art of rhetoric was divided into five areas: *inventio, dispositio, elocutio* or *decoratio, memoria,* and *pronunciatio; inventio* entailed finding the subject matter, and in *dispositio,* the material was ordered or arranged to serve the writer's purposes; once the material was arranged, *elocutio* involved amplifying and decorating the poetry with fine words and sentences; the discourse then was memorized *(memoria)* and delivered, *pronunciatio* being concerned with the techniques of delivery orators employed to move the passions of listeners.
schemes	a class of figures which removes language from the common custom by creating highly artificial patterns of speech (for example, repetitions of all sorts) (Peacham the Elder 1577 f E1v)
sensable figures	figures which stir the mind by altering conceit or sense (Puttenham 1589 pp 171–2, 188–9)
sententious figures	figures designed 'all at once to beautifie and geve sence and sententiousnes to the whole language at large' (stirring the mind while delighting the ear) (Puttenham 1589 p 206)
subjection	a figure in which several questions are asked and answers are given to each one of them (Le Faucheur 1657 p 144)
symploche	a figure which occurs 'when one and the selfe [same] word doth begin and end many verses in sute' (Puttenham 1589 p 209)

synathroismos	a figure which involves 'a multiplication or heaping togeather of manye wordes, sygnifyinge dyvers thinges of like nature' (Peacham the Elder 1577 f Q2r)
syncopatio catachrestica	an irrregular resolution of a suspension (Bernhard p 77; trans Hilse 1973 pp 102–3)
syncope	a suspension (Bartel 1985 pp 262–9)
synonymia	rhetoric: a figure designed to make the sense stronger and more obvious by using words which differ from the preceding ones in form or sound but which mean the same (Sherry 1550 p 49, Peacham the Elder 1577 f P4r, Puttenham 1589 p 223)
	music: the repetition of a melodic fragment at a different pitch level (but not one step higher or lower)
tropes	a class of figures which serve to alter the signification of a word or words from the normal meaning to something not proper but quite close (for example, metaphor) (Peacham the Elder 1577 f B1v)
zeugma	a figure in which a single word serves more than one clause; if the common servitor appears in the first clause of a series, it is called *prozeugma* (Puttenham 1589 pp 175–6).

# BIBLIOGRAPHY

Selected Primary Sources

Ascham 1545   Ascham, Roger. *Toxophilus, The schole of shootinge.*
London 1545; facs Amsterdam 1969

Attey 1622   Attey, John. *The First Booke of Ayres.* London 1622

Bacon 1627   Bacon, Francis. *Sylva sylvarum.* London 1627

Bartlet 1606   Bartlet, John. *A Booke of Ayres.* London 1606

Barton 1634   Barton, John. *The Art of Rhetorick Concisely and Compleatly
Handled.* London 1634

Bassano 1585   Bassano, Giovanni. *Ricercate, passaggi et cadentie.* Venice
1585

Bassano 1591   — *Motetti, madrigali et canzoni francese.* Venice 1591

Bathe 1587   Bathe, William. *A Briefe Introduction to the skill of song.*
London ca 1587; facs Kilkenny 1982

Bernhard   Bernhard, Christoph. *Tractatus compositionis augmentatus.*
In *Die Kompositionslehre Heinrich Schützens in der
Fassung seines Schülers Christoph Bernhard* ed Joseph
M. Müller-Blattau (Leipzig 1963)

Bevin 1631   Bevin, Elway. *A Briefe and Short Instruction of the Art of
Musicke.* London 1631

Bovicelli 1594   Bovicelli, Giovanni. *Regole, passaggi di musica.* Venice
1594

Brinsley 1612   Brinsley, John. *Ludus literarius: or, The Grammar Schoole.*
London 1612

Brinsley 1622	— *A Consolation for our Grammar Schooles*. London 1622; facs Amsterdam 1969
Bulwer 1644	Bulwer, John. *Chirologia: or the Naturall Language of the Hand ... Chironomia: or the Art of Manuall Rhetorike*. London 1644. Ed James W. Cleary (Carbondale 1974)
Burmeister 1606	Burmeister, Joachim. *Musica poetica*. Rostock 1606
Butler 1633	Butler, Charles. *The English Grammar*. Oxford 1633
Butler 1636	— *The Principles of Musik*. London 1636; facs Amsterdam 1970
Byrd 1588	Byrd, William. *Psalmes, sonets, & songs of sadnes and pietie*. London 1588
Caccini 1601	Caccini, Giulio. *Le nuove musiche*. Florence 1601. Ed H. Wiley Hitchcock (Madison 1970)
	Cambridge, Fitzwilliam Museum. Ms Mu 782 (formerly ms 52.D.25)
	Cambridge, King's College Library. Rowe ms 2
Campion 1601	Songs in Rosseter 1601
Campion 1602	Campion, Thomas. *Observations in the art of English Poesie*. London 1602
Campion 1607	— *The Discription of a Maske ... in Honour of the Lord Hayes*. London 1607
Campion 1610	— *A new way of making fowre parts*. London 1610
Campion 1613/1	— *Two Bookes of Ayres, The First*. London ca 1613
Campion 1613/2	— *Two Bookes of Ayres, The Second*. London ca 1613
Campion 1613/3	— *A Relation of the late Royall Entertainment ... at Cawsome-House*. London 1613
Campion 1614	— *The Description of a Maske ... At the Mariage of the Right Honourable the Earl of Somerset*. London 1614
Campion 1618/3	— *The Third and Fourth Booke of Ayres*. [The Third] London ca 1618
Campion 1618/4	— *The Third and Fourth Booke of Ayres*. [The Fourth] London ca 1618
Case 1586	Case, John. *The Praise of Musicke*. London 1586
Case 1588	— *Apologia Musices*. London 1588
Cavalieri 1600	Cavalieri, Emilio de'. *Rappresentatione di anima, et di corpo*. Rome 1600; facs Farnborough 1967
Cavendish 1598	Cavendish, Michaell. *14 Ayres*. London 1598

Clement 1587   Clement, Francis. *The Petie Schole*. London 1587; facs in
                    Pepper 1966

Cooke 1640   Cooke, Walter. *A briefe sume of the Arts of Logick,*
                    Sophistry, and Rhetorick. Oxford, Bodleian Library,
                    ms Ashmole 768, pp 492–541, ?after 1640?

Coprario 1606   Coprario, John. *Funeral Teares*. London 1606

Coprario 1613   — *Songs of Mourning*. London 1613

Corkine 1610   Corkine, William. *Ayres*. London 1610

Corkine 1612   — *The Second Booke of Ayres*. London 1612

dalla Casa 1584   dalla Casa, Girolamo. *Il vero modo di diminuir*. Venice 1584

Danyel 1606   Danyel, John. *Songs for the Lute, Viol and Voice*. London
                    1606

del Lago 1540   del Lago, Giovanni. *Breve introduttione di musica misura-*
                    ta. Venice 1540; facs Bologna 1969

Dowland 1597   Dowland, John. *The First Booke of Songes or Ayres*. London
                    1597 and subsequent editions in 1600, 1603, 1606,
                    1613

Dowland 1600   — *The Second Booke of Songs or Ayres*. London 1600

Dowland 1603   — *The Third and Last Booke of Songs or Aires*. London
                    1603

Dowland 1609   — *Andreas Ornithoparcus His Micrologus, or Introduction:*
                    Containing the Art of Singing. London 1609; facs New
                    York 1973

Dowland 1612   — *A Pilgrimes Solace*. London 1612

Dowland (R) 1610   Dowland, Robert. *A Musicall Banquet*. London 1610
                    Dublin, Trinity College Library. Ms F.5.13

Elyot 1546   Elyot, Thomas. *The Boke Named the Governour*. London
                    1546

Fenner 1584   Fenner, Dudley. *The Artes of Logike and Rhetorike*.
                    Middleburg 1584; facs in Pepper 1966

Ferrabosco 1609   Ferrabosco, Alfonso. *Ayres*. London 1609

Finck 1556   Finck, Hermann. *Practica musica*. Wittenberg 1556; facs
                    Bologna 1969

Flud 1617   Flud, Robert. *Utriusque cosmi*. London 1617

Ford 1607   Ford, Thomas. *Musicke of Sundrie Kindes*. London 1607

Fraunce 1588   Fraunce, Abraham. *The Arcadian Rhetorike*. London 1588;
                    facs Menston 1969

Gil 1619   Gil, Alexander. *Logonomia Anglica*. London 1619

Granger 1616   Granger, Thomas. *Syntagma Grammaticum.* London
                      1616; facs Menston 1971

Greaves 1604   Greaves, Thomas. *Songes of Sundrie Kindes.* London 1604

Greene 1615   [Greene, John.] *A Refutation of the Apology for Actors.*
                      London 1615; facs New York 1973

Hart 1551   Hart, John. *The Opening of the Unreasonable Writing of our
                      Inglish Toung* (1551). In *John Hart's Works on English
                      Orthography and Pronunciation* ed Bror Danielsson
                      (Stockholm 1955)

Hart 1569   — *An Orthographie* (1569). In *John Hart's Works on
                      English Orthography and Pronunciation* ed Bror
                      Danielsson (Stockholm 1955)

Hertford 1591   Hertford, Earl of. *The Honorable Entertainement gieven to
                      the Queenes Maiestie in Progresse, at Elvetham in
                      Hampshire, by the right Honorable the Earle of Hertford
                      1591.* London 1591

Heywood 1612   Heywood, Thomas. *An Apology for Actors.* London 1612;
                      facs New York 1973

Hobbes 1637   Hobbes, Thomas. *A Briefe of the Art of Rhetorique.*
                      London 1637. In *The Rhetorics of Thomas Hobbes and
                      Bernard Lamy* ed John T. Harwood (Carbondale
                      1986)

Hooker 1597   Hooker, Richard. *Of the Lawes of Ecclesiasticall Politie, The
                      fift Booke.* London 1597; facs Amsterdam 1971

Hoskins 1599   Hoskins, John. *Direccōns for Speech and Style* (1599). In
                      *The Life, Letters, and Writings of John Hoskyns
                      1566–1638* ed Louise B. Osborn (Hamden 1973)

Jones 1600   Jones, Robert. *The First Booke of Songes or Ayres.* London
                      1600

Jones 1601   — *The Second Booke of Songs and Ayres.* London 1601

Jones 1605   — *Ultimum Vale.* London 1605

Jones 1609   — *A Musicall Dreame.* London 1609

Jones 1610   — *The Muses Gardin for Delights.* London 1610

Kempe 1588   Kempe, William. *The Education of Children in Learning.*
                      London 1588; facs in Pepper 1966

Le Faucheur 1657   Le Faucheur, Michel. *Traitte de l'action de l'orateur ou de
                      la Prononciation et du geste.* Paris 1657. Trans as *An
                      Essay upon the Action of an Orator, as to his Pronun-
                      ciation and Gesture.* London ?1680? or ?1700?

Lily 1567	Lily, William. *Brevissima institutio*. London 1567; facs New York 1945
	London, British Library. Mss Add 15117, 24665, 29481, 3140; Egerton 2971
	Los Angeles, William Andrews Clark Memorial Library. The Mansell Lyra Viol Tablature
Mace 1676	Mace, Thomas. *Musick's Monument*. London 1676; facs Paris 1958
	Manchester, Public Library. Watson Collection, ms 832 Vu 51
Mason 1618	Mason, George and John Earsden. *The Ayres that were Sung and Played at Brougham Castle*. London 1618
Maynard 1611	Maynard, John. *The XII Wonders of the World*. London 1611
Morley 1597	Morley, Thomas. *A Plaine and Easie Introduction to Practicall Musicke*. London 1597; facs Amsterdam 1969
Morley 1600	— *The First Booke of Ayres*. London 1600
Mulcaster 1581	Mulcaster, Richard. *Positions*. London 1581; facs Amsterdam 1971
Mulcaster 1582	— *Elementarie*. London 1582. Ed E.T. Campagnac as *Mulcaster's Elementarie* (Oxford 1925)
Notari 1613	Notari, Angelo. *Prime musiche nuove*. London 1613
Nucius 1613	Nucius, Johannes. *Musices poeticae*. Neisse 1613
Ortiz 1553	Ortiz, Diego. *Trattado de glosas sobre clausulas*. Rome 1553
	Oxford, Bodleian Library. Mss Tenbury 1018, 1019
	Oxford, Christ Church Library. Mss 87, 439
Peacham the Elder 1577	Peacham, Henry. *The Garden of Eloquence*. London 1577; facs Menston 1971
Peacham the Elder 1593	Peacham, Henry. *The Garden of Eloquence*. London 1593; facs Gainesville 1954
Peacham the Younger 1622	Peacham, Henry. *The Compleat Gentleman*. London 1622; facs Amsterdam 1968
Pilkington 1605	Pilkington, Francis. *The First Booke of Songs or Ayres*. London 1605
Playford 1655	Playford, John. *An Introduction to the Skill of Musick*. London 1655
Praetorius 1619	Praetorius, Michael. *Syntagma musicum, tomus tertius*. Wolfenbüttel 1619; facs Kassel 1958

Puttenham 1589	Puttenham, George. *The Arte of English Poesie*. London 1589. Ed Baxter Hathaway (Kent 1970)
Quintilian	Quintilian. *The Institutio Oratoria of Quintilian*. Ed and trans H.E. Butler (London 1920–2)
Ravenscroft 1614	Ravenscroft, Thomas. *A Briefe Discourse*. London 1614
Ravenscroft Ms	— *Treatise of Musicke*. London, British Library, ms Add 19,758
Rhetorica	Anon. *Rhetorica ad Herennium*. Ed and trans Harry Caplan (London 1954)
Robinson 1641	[Robinson, Ralph.] *An English Grammar*. London 1641; facs Menston 1972
Robinson (T) 1603	Robinson, Thomas. *The Schoole of Musicke*. London 1603; facs Amsterdam 1973
Rognioni 1620	Rognioni, Francesco. *Selva di varii passaggi*. Milan 1620
Rogniono 1592	Rogniono, Richardo. *Passaggi*. Venice 1592
Rosseter 1601	Rosseter, Philip. *A Booke of Ayres*. London 1601
Shakespeare 1623	Shakespeare, William. *Mr. William Shakespeares Comedies, Histories, & Tragedies*. London 1623
Sherry 1550	Sherry, Richard. *A Treatise of Schemes and Tropes*. London 1550; facs Gainesville 1961
Simpson 1665	Simpson, Christopher. *The Division Viol*. London 1665
Smith 1657	Smith, John. *The Mysterie of Rhetorique Unvail'd*. London 1657; facs Hildesheim 1973
Vicentino 1555	Vicentino, Nicola. *L'antica musica ridotta alla moderna prattica*. Rome 1555; facs Kassel 1959
Walther 1708	Walther, Johann G. *Praecepta der Musicalischen Composition*. Ed Peter Benary (Leipzig 1955)
Webbe 1586	Webbe, William. *A Discourse of English Poetrie*. London 1586
Wilbye 1609	Wilbye, John. *The second set of madrigales*. London 1609
Wilson 1553	Wilson, Thomas. *The Arte of Rhetorique*. London 1553. Ed Thomas J. Derrick (New York 1982)
Wright 1604	Wright, Thomas. *The Passions of the Minde in Generall*. London 1604; facs of the 1630 ed Urbana 1971
Zarlino 1558	Zarlino, Gioseffo. *Le istitutioni harmoniche*. Venice 1558; facs New York 1965
Zarlino 1588	— *Sopplimenti musicali*. Venice 1588; facs Ridgewood 1966

Selected Secondary Literature

Austern 1985	Austern, Linda P. 'Sweet Meats with Sour Sauce: The Genesis of Musical Irony in English Drama after 1600.' *Journal of Musicology* 4 (1985–6) 472–90
Baldwin 1944	Baldwin, Thomas W. *William Shakespere's Small Latine and Lesse Greeke*, 2 vols. Urbana 1944
Barnett 1987	Barnett, Dene. *The Art of Gesture: The Practices and Principles of 18th-Century Acting.* Heidelberg 1987
Bartel 1985	Bartel, Dietrich. *Handbuch der musikalischen Figurenlehre.* Laaber 1985
Brett 1967	Brett, Philip. *Consort Songs. Musica Britannica* 22. London 1967
Brett 1989	— *The Byrd Edition*, vol 5 (Gradualia I [1605], The Marian Masses). London 1989
Brown 1973–4	Brown, Howard M. 'Embellishment in early Sixteenth-Century Italian Intabulations.' *Proceedings of the Royal Musical Association* 100 (1973–4) 49–83
Brown 1976	— *Embellishing Sixteenth-Century Music.* Oxford 1976
Brown 1982	— 'Emulation, Competition, and Homage: Imitation and Theories of Imitation in the Renaissance.' *Journal of the American Musicological Society* 35 (1982) 1–48
Buelow 1980	Buelow, George J. 'Rhetoric and Music.' *New Grove* 15: 793–803
Butler 1980	Butler, Gregory. 'Music and Rhetoric in Early Seventeenth-Century English Sources.' *Musical Quarterly* 66 (1980) 53–64
Clark 1979	Clark, J. Bunker. *Nathaniel Giles: Anthems. Early English Church Music* 23. London 1979
Collingwood 1961	Collingwood, Robin G. *The Idea of History.* London 1961
Colson 1924	Colson, Francis H. *M. Fabii Quintiliani Institutionis Oratoriae.* Cambridge 1924
Conley 1990	Conley, Thomas M. *Rhetoric in the European Tradition.* New York 1990
Crane 1960	Crane, Frederick. 'A Study of Theoretical Writings on Musical Form to *ca.* 1460.' PHD diss, University of Iowa, 1960
Cutts 1959	Cutts, John P. '"M[ris] Elizabeth Davenant 1624" Christ

	Church MS. Mus. 87.' *Review of English Studies* 10 (1959) 26–37
Cyr 1971	Cyr, Mary. 'A Seventeenth-Century Source of Ornamentation for Voice and Viol: British Museum Ms. Egerton 2971.' *Royal Musical Association Research Chronicle* 9 (1971) 53–72
Dart 1961	Dart, Thurston. 'Ornament Signs in Jacobean Music for Lute and Viol.' *Galpin Society Journal* 14 (1961) 30–3
Dobson 1968	Dobson, Eric J. *English Pronunciation, 1500–1700*, 2 vols. Oxford 1968
Doughtie 1970	Doughtie, Edward. *Lyrics from English Airs 1596–1622*. Cambridge, Mass 1970
Doughtie 1986	— *English Renaissance Song*. Boston 1986
Duckles 1957	Duckles, Vincent. 'Florid Embellishment in English Song of the Late 16th and Early 17th Centuries.' *Annales Musicologiques* 5 (1957) 329–45
Elders 1981	Elders, Willem. 'Guillaume Dufay as Musical Orator.' *Tijdschrift van de Vereniging voor Nederlandse Muziekgeschiedenis* 31 (1981) 1–15
Erig 1979	Erig, Richard. *Italienische Diminutionen*. Zurich 1979
Evans 1987	Evans, G. Blakemore. *Elizabethan-Jacobean Drama*. London 1987
Feldman 1987	Feldman, Martha. 'In Defense of Campion: A New Look at his Ayres and *Observations*.' *Journal of Musicology* 5 (1987) 226–56
Fenlon 1982	Fenlon, Iain, ed. *Cambridge Music Manuscripts, 900–1700*. Cambridge 1982
Greer 1987	Greer, David. *Collected English Lutenist Partsongs. Musica Britannica* 53, 54. London 1987–9
Gurr 1970	Gurr, Andrew. *The Shakespearean Stage 1574–1642*. Cambridge 1970
Hankey 1981	Hankey, Susan. 'The Compleat Gentleman's Music.' *Music and Letters* 62 (1981) 146–54
Hattaway 1982	Hattaway, Michael. *Elizabethan Popular Theatre, Plays in Performance*. London 1982
Hilse 1973	Hilse, Walter, trans. 'The Treatises of Christoph Bernhard.' *The Music Forum* 3 (1973) 1–196
Houston 1983	Houston, John P. *The Rhetoric of Poetry in the Renaissance and Seventeenth Century*. Baton Rouge 1983

Howell 1961	Howell, Wilbur S. *Logic and Rhetoric in England, 1500–1700*. New York 1961
Joiner 1969	Joiner, Mary. 'British Museum Add Ms. 15117: A Commentary, Index and Bibliography.' *Royal Musical Association Research Chronicle* 7 (1969) 51–109
Jones 1989	Jones, Edward H. *The Performance of English Song 1610–1670*. New York 1989
Jorgens 1982	Jorgens, Elise B. *The Well-Tun'd Word, Musical Interpretations of English Poetry 1597–1651*. Minneapolis 1982
Jorgens 1986–9	— ed. *English Song 1600–1675*, 12 vols. New York 1986–9
Joseph 1951	Joseph, Bertram. *Elizabethan Acting*. London 1951; 2nd ed 1964
Joseph 1960	— *Acting Shakespeare*. London 1960
Joseph 1983	— 'The Dramatic and Rhetorical Speaker's "Person" and "Action" in the English Renaissance.' In *Performance of Literature in Historical Perspectives* ed David W. Thompson (Lanham 1983) 459–75
Kenyon 1988	Kenyon, Nicholas, ed. *Authenticity and Early Music, A Symposium*. Oxford 1988
Lanham 1968	Lanham, Richard. *A Handlist of Rhetorical Terms*. Berkeley 1968
Lanham 1976	— *The Motives of Eloquence*. New Haven 1976
LeCoat 1975	LeCoat, Gerard. *The Rhetoric of the Arts, 1550–1650*. Bern 1975
Leech-Wilkinson 1991	Leech-Wilkinson, Daniel. 'My Lady's Tears: A Pair of Songs by John Dowland.' *Early Music* 19 (1991) 227–33
MacClintock 1979	MacClintock, Carol. *Readings in the History of Music in Performance*. Bloomington 1979
Mackerness 1964	Mackerness, E.D. *A Social History of English Music*. London 1964
Maniates 1983	Maniates, Maria R. 'Music and Rhetoric: Facets of Cultural History in the Renaissance and the Baroque.' *Israel Studies in Musicology* 3 (1983) 44–69
Marriott 1979	Mariott, David. 'English Lute Ornamentation.' *Guitar and Lute* 9 (1979) 30–3; 10 (1979) 25–8
Mellers 1965	Mellers, Wilfrid. *Harmonious Meeting*. London 1965
Meyer 1969	Meyer, Sam. 'The Figures of Rhetoric in Spenser's *Colin*

	Clout.' In *Rhetorical Analyses of Literary Works* ed Edward P.J. Corbett (New York 1969) 147–75
Mohrmann 1983	Mohrmann, Gerald P. 'Oratorical Delivery and Other Problems in Current Scholarship on English Renaissance Rhetoric.' In Murphy 1983 pp 56–83
Murphy 1983	Murphy, James J., ed. *Renaissance Eloquence, Studies in the Theory and Practice of Renaissance Rhetoric.* Berkeley 1983
Oboussier 1953	Oboussier, Philippe. 'Turpyn's Book of Lute-Songs.' *Music and Letters* 34 (1953) 145–9
Palisca 1972	Palisca, Claude V. '*Ut oratoria musica:* The Rhetorical Basis of Musical Mannerism.' In *The Meaning of Mannerism* ed Franklin W. Robinson and Stephen G. Nichols (Hanover, NH 1972) 37–65
Pattison 1970	Pattison, Bruce. *Music and Poetry of the English Renaissance.* London 1970
Pepper 1966	Pepper, Robert. *Four Tudor Books on Education.* Gainesville 1966
Poulton 1975	Poulton, Diana. 'Graces of Play in Renaissance Lute Music.' *Early Music* 3 (1975) 107–14
Poulton 1980	— 'Rosseter, Philip.' *New Grove* 16: 211–12
Poulton 1982	— *John Dowland,* 2nd ed. London 1982
Price 1981	Price, David C. *Patrons and Musicians of the English Renaissance.* Cambridge 1981
Rastall 1973	Rastall, Richard. Introduction to *The Turpyn Book of Lute Songs.* Leeds 1973
Ratcliffe 1981	Ratcliffe, Stephen. *Campion: On Song.* Boston 1981
Rix 1940	Rix, Herbert D. *Rhetoric in Spenser's Poetry.* State College, Pa 1940
Rooley 1983	Rooley, Anthony. 'New Light on John Dowland's Songs of Darkness.' *Early Music* 11 (1983) 6–21
Scott 1979a	Scott, David. *Thomas Campion, First Book of Ayres.* London 1979
Scott 1979b	— *Thomas Campion, Second Book of Ayres.* London 1979
Shapiro 1977	Shapiro, Michael. *Children of the Revels, The Boy Companies of Shakespeare's Time and Their Plays.* New York 1977
Sister Joseph 1947	Joseph, Sister Miriam. *Shakespeare's Use of the Arts of Language.* New York 1947

Smith 1973 — Smith, James. 'John Dowland: A Reappraisal of His Ayres.' DMA diss, University of Illinois at Urbana, 1973

Sonnino 1968 — Sonnino, Lee A. *A Handbook to Sixteenth-Century Rhetoric*. London 1968

Spencer 1976 — Spencer, Robert. *The Board Lute Book*. Leeds 1976

Spencer 1984 — — 'Performance Style of the English Lute Ayre c. 1600.' *The Lute, The Journal of the Lute Society* 24 (1984) 55–68

Spink 1966 — Spink, Ian. 'Sources of English Song, 1620–1660: A Survey.' *Miscellanea Musicologica* 1 (1966) 117–36

Spink 1986 — — *English Song Dowland to Purcell*. London 1974; repr with corrections 1986

Swanekamp 1984 — Swanekamp, Joan. *English Ayres, A Selectively Annotated Bibliography and Discography*. Westport 1984

Till 1975 — Till, David. 'Ornamentation in English Song Manuscripts 1620–1660.' BLITT thesis, University of Oxford, 1975

Toft 1984 — Toft, Robert. 'Musicke a sister to Poetrie: Rhetorical Artifice in the Passionate Airs of John Dowland.' *Early Music* 12 (1984) 190–9

Tomlinson 1984 — Tomlinson, Gary. 'The Web of Culture: A Context for Musicology.' *19th-Century Music* 7 (1984) 350–62

Tomlinson 1988 — — 'The Historian, the Performer, and Authentic Meaning in Music.' In Kenyon 1988 pp 115–36

Unger 1941 — Unger, Hans-Heinrich. *Die Beziehungen zwischen Musik und Rhetorik im 16.–18. Jahrhundert*. Würzburg 1941; repr Hildesheim 1982

Vickers 1982 — Vickers, Brian. 'On the Practicalities of Renaissance Rhetoric.' In *Rhetoric Revalued* ed Brian Vickers (Binghamton 1982) 133–41

Vickers 1983 — — '"The Power of Persuasion": Images of the Orator, Elyot to Shakespeare.' In Murphy 1983 pp 411–35

Vickers 1984 — — 'Figures of Rhetoric/Figures of Music?' *Rhetorica* 2 (1984) 1–44

Vickers 1988 — — *In Defence of Rhetoric*. Oxford 1988

Vickers 1989 — — *Classical Rhetoric in English Poetry*. Carbondale 1989

Walls 1984 — Walls, Peter. '"Music and Sweet Poetry"? Verse for English Lute Song and Continuo Song.' *Music and Letters* 65 (1984) 237–54

Ward 1977   Ward, John. 'A Dowland Miscellany.' *Journal of the Lute Society of America* 10 (1977) 5–153

Wells 1974   Wells, Robin H. 'The Art of Persuasion: A Note on the Lyric 'Come again: sweet love doth now invite' from Dowland's *First Book of Airs*.' *Lute Society Journal* 16 (1974) 67–9

Wells 1984   — 'The Ladder of Love, Verbal and Musical Rhetoric in the Elizabethan Lute-Song.' *Early Music* 12 (1984) 173–89

Wells 1985   — 'John Dowland and Elizabethan Melancholy.' *Early Music* 13 (1985) 514–28

Wells 1989   — 'Ars Amatoria: Philip Rosseter and the Tudor Court Lyric.' *Music and Letters* 70 (1989) 58–71

Wilson 1989   Wilson, Christopher R. *Words and Notes Coupled Lovingly Together: Thomas Campion, a Critical Study*. New York 1989

Wilson 1991   — Review of *The Life and Works of Philip Rosseter* by John Jeffreys. *Music and Letters* 72 (1991) 580–1

Winn 1981   Winn, James A. *Unsuspected Eloquence*. New Haven 1981

Woodfill 1953   Woodfill, Walter L. *Musicians in English Society from Elizabeth to Charles I*. Princeton 1953

Wulstan 1985   Wulstan, David. *Tudor Music*. London 1985

✦ LIST OF EXAMPLES

Chapter 1   *Elocutio*

Chapter 2   *Pronunciatio*

Chapter 3   *Passionate Ayres Pronounced*

INDEX

9 781487 573546